TWAYNE'S WORLD AUTHORS SERIES
A Survey of the World's Literature

Sylvia E. Bowman, Indiana University

GENERAL EDITOR

FRANCE

Maxwell A. Smith, Guerry Professor of French, Emeritus
The University of Chattanooga
Former Visiting Professor in Modern Languages
The Florida State University

EDITOR

René Char

TWAS 428

Photo credit: Peter Caws, 1975

René Char

RENÉ CHAR

By MARY ANN CAWS

Hunter College and
The Graduate Center of the
City University of New York

TWAYNE PUBLISHERS
A DIVISION OF G. K. HALL & CO., BOSTON

Library of Congress Cataloging in Publication Data

Caws, Mary Ann.
    René Char.

    (Twayne's world authors series ; TWAS 428 : France)
    Bibliography: p. 163–68.
    Includes index.
    1.   Char, René, 1907–   2.   Authors, French—
20th century—Biography.
PQ2605.H3345Z633   848'.9'1209   76–50031
ISBN   0–8057–6268–X

for Hilary and Matthew

. . . d'immenses perspectives de poésie . . .
Partage formel

Contents

About the Author

Professor of Romance Languages and Comparative Literature at Hunter College and at the Graduate Center of the City University of New York, Mary Ann Caws is in charge of the Doctoral Program in Comparative Literature. She has been Visiting Professor at Princeton University, President of the Association for the Study of Dada and Surrealism, has judged translations for the National Book Awards, has held fellowships and grants from the Guggenheim Foundation, the Senior Fulbright-Hays Program, and the National Endowment for the Humanities, and is a member of the Executive Council of the Modern Language Association.

Professor Caws is the author of *Surrealism and the Literary Imagination, The Poetry of Dada and Surrealism, André Breton, The Inner Theater of Recent French Poetry, The Surrealist Voice of Robert Desnos,* and *The Presence of René Char.* She edited and translated *Approximate Man and Other Writings of Tristan Tzara* and translated and annotated, with Jonathan Griffin, *Poems of René Char.* She is the editor of *About French Poetry from Dada to Tel Quel: Text and Theory,* and of the journals *Dada/Surrealism* and *Le Siècle éclaté: études sur dada, le surréalisme et les avant-gardes.*

Preface

The case of René Char is singular in all senses of the word. For the critic who wishes neither to be swayed by the personality of the author nor to overlook it in discussing the work, the responsibility of a judicious presentation is a difficult one. More than any other French poet of our time, Char dominates his place and his moment, invalidating any possible label or rubric. This is not merely the subjective view of the present writer: all the testimonies agree on this point. The testimonies and what occasions them have not changed over the years: Char is now, at the moment of this writing, in his late sixties. I can only hope that the effort implicit in the attempt at a relatively dispassionate analysis will lend its tension to the style of and its intensity to the thought behind this essay, in which the guiding theme is the relation between a life, a text, and a countryside — interior and exterior — and between a poetics and a morality whose origin is specific and whose application is wide-ranging.

This book represents also a rereading, after *The Presence of René Char* (Princeton, 1976)[1] and the translations of the *Poems of René Char* (Princeton, 1976). The present essay is intended to be more open in its writing and more inclusive in its approach than the former book, which was a deliberately elliptical rendering of one reader's reaction to a poet's work and presence. Yet, like the concept of exterior and interior geography at the heart of this work, the two series of readings — each representing a lengthy immersion in the texts — are meant to correspond, not in the outer and obvious sense, but rather by an intuitive and interior passage.

MARY ANN CAWS

The Graduate Center of the
City University of New York

Acknowledgements

The preliminary study for this book was supported by a grant from the National Endowment for the Humanities and then by a Faculty Research Award from the City University of New York.

Some of the analyses are based on manuscripts consulted in the Fonds René Char-Yvonne Zervos in the Bibliothèque littéraire Jacques Doucet: my thanks to François Chapon for his helpfulness. To Tina Jolas, and to Peter Caws, I am continually indebted for their suggestions and their encouragement. My warmest gratitude to René Char.

My grateful appreciation for the permission to quote from the following works by René Char: José Corti, for "Voici," from *Le Marteau sans maître* (c) 1970; to Editions Gallimard for "Fréquence," from *Fureur et mystère* (c) 1962; for "Marmonnement," from *Les Matinaux, suivi de La Parole en archipel* (c) 1962, and for "Tracé sur le gouffre," *"Enchemisé dans les violences...,"* "L'Abri rudoyé," and "Joie," from *Le Nu perdu* (c) 1971; to the Princeton University Press for permission to use the quotations in English from *Poems of René Char,* translated and annotated by Mary Ann Caws and Jonathan Griffin, Princeton, 1976. The translations marked [JG] are Jonathan Griffin's; all others are my own. N. B. With the exception of the complete poems listed above, the quotations are excerpts and must be read as such.

Chronology

1907   Birth at L'Isle-sur-Sorgue, Vaucluse, in South of France.
1928   *Les Cloches sur le coeur,* written between 1922–1926, under the name René-Emile Char.
1929   *Arsenal;* Char sends copy to Eluard, who comes to L'Isle. Char meets with Surrealist group in Paris.
1930   *Ralentir travaux* (in collaboration with Breton and Eluard). *Artine.*
1931   *L'Action de la justice est éteinte.*
1934   *Le Marteau sans maître* (collected edition).
1935   Separation from Surrealist group.
1937   *Placard pour un chemin des écoliers,* illustrated by Valentine Hugo.
1938   *Dehors la nuit est gouvernée.*
1939–   War in Alsace. Subsequently, "Capitaine Alexandre" in
1945   the Resistance; regional head of a partisan group in the Alpes-de-Provence. In July 1944, ordered to Algiers on an advisory mission to the Supreme Allied Headquarters.
1945   *Seuls demeurent* (collected edition).
1946   *Feuillets d'Hypnos. Le Poème pulvérisé.*
1948   *Fureur et mystère* (collected edition).
1949   *Le Soleil des eaux,* illustrated by Braque.
1950   *Les Matinaux* (collected edition).
1951   *A une sérénité crispée.*
1952   *La Paroi et la prairie.*
        Le Rempart de brindilles, illustrated by Wifredo Lam.
1954   *A la santé du serpent,* illustrated by Miró.
1955   *Recherche de la base et du sommet,* followed by *Pauvreté et privilège* (collected edition of prose texts).
1956   *Les Compagnons dans le jardin,* illustrated by Zao Wou-Ki.
1957   *Poèmes et prose choisis* (collected edition).
1960   *L'Inclémence lointaine,* illustrated by Vieira da Silva.
1962   *La Parole en archipel* (collected edition).
1963   *Lettera amorosa,* illustrated by Braque.

RENÉ CHAR

1964   *Commune présence* (anthology).
1965   *Retour amont,* illustrated by Giacometti.
1967   *Trois coups sous les arbres: Théâtre saisonnier* (collected edition of theater). *Les Transparents,* illustrated by Picasso.
1968   *Dans la pluie giboyeuse.*
1971   *L'Effroi la joie,* illustrated by Sima.
       Exposition René Char at Fondation Maeght and Musée d'Art moderne de la Ville de Paris, *Catalogue-Anthologie.*
1972   *Le Nu perdu* (collected edition). *La Nuit talismanique,* illustrated by the poet.
1975   *Le Monde de l'art n'est pas le monde du pardon* (texts on and for painters; illustrations by Klee, Kandinsky, Villeri, Braque, Matisse, Jean Hugo, N. de Staël, Brauner, Fernandez, Grenier, Charbonnier, Miró, Lam, Reichek,. Char, Picasso, Zao Wou-Ki, Vieira da Silva, Giacometti, Szenes, Sima, Boyan, Pierre-André Benoit; preface by Jacques Dupin).
1975   *Aromates chasseurs.*

CHAPTER 1

Poetics and Morality

I Life and Early Text

IN his preface to *La Nuit talismanique (Talismanic Night)* Char describes the psychological atmosphere of his childhood, presenting an unforgettable picture of his parents: "My father had courteous, shining eyes, good and never possessive.... My mother seemed to touch everything and to reach nothing, at once busy, indolent, and sure of herself. The strong lines of their contrasting natures clashed with each other, their intersection catching fire." (*La Nuit talismanique,* p. 9)[1] The ten year old saw his father returning more and more exhausted each evening from the family plaster factory: he died after a long illness, in which "a forest of oaks was burned in the fireplace." From the powerful effect of this page, one gesture stands out: the father laying his hand on the boy's shoulder with a weight which seems to carry into the present. And in one portrait by Hierlé, the father's look seems to show a similar extension into the time of our reading: Char points out "in the present of his gaze a dream which is not his alone, but whose listener we are together" (NT, 9).

I shall sketch rapidly the few lines of Char's history which are essential, and of which each reader is himself a listener, together now with the poet. Then the poetry takes its own route with its own marked and unmarked points, according to an interior dynamics of its own, in the spirit of Char's definition:

Le poème est l'amour réalisé du désir demeuré désir.
The poem is the fulfilled love of desire as it remains desire. (*Sur la poésie,* p. 10)[2]

For enthusiasts of biographical and geographical anecdote, there is no dearth of detail. For example, the poem "Jouvence des

13

Névons" recounts the poet's childhood in a deserted village where the men are away at war. "The child, a stream, and a rebellious nature converge in one single being, modified according to the years. It shines and fades by turn, according to the event, on the horizon's steps" (*Les Matinaux* [*The Matinals*], 1st ed).[3] Accompanying the scene, a cricket is still and yet all the more present for its stillness. The tone of that one poem could be considered characteristic of much of Char's writing, whether it deals with childhood, adolescence, manhood, or an advancing age: personal and vaguely mysterious, placed in a distant time and yet informing the moment of writing and all the subsequent moments of reading.

From the next period comes the collection *Arsenal,* of major importance for the understanding of the poet's future work. A copy of the collection was given to Eluard,[4] whose enthusiasm caused him to present Char to the Surrealist group, with which Char was associated from 1930–1934, the period of *Artine* and the poems in *Abondance viendra* (*Abundance will come*), among others. From this arsenal, where sufficient weapons for all future skirmishes are stored, we might consider just the poem "Voici" ("Here is") as an example of the possible interior linking of life and text.

> Voici l'écumeur de mémoire
> Le vapeur des flaques mineures
> Entouré de linges fumants
> Etoile rose et rose blanche
>
> O caresses savantes, ô lèvres inutiles!
>
> Here is memory's plunderer
> The mist of minor pools
> Surrounded by steaming linen
> Rose star and white rose
>
> Oh knowing caresses, oh useless lips!

(*Le Marteau sans maître* [*The Hammer with No Master*], p. 30)[5]

If we compare this text with a far longer one from *Le Tombeau des secrets* (*The Tomb of Secrets*) (an early volume, some of whose few poems are taken up and revised in *Arsenal*), the difference is startling, seemingly indicative of a sharp reduction in sentimentality. This particular development will determine the course of much of

Char's writing and of his life, in both of which the containing force of the personality prevents any prolonged lapse into self-pity or any tendency to shed *lacrimae rerum* either from nostalgia or from a lucid observation of the world around. As is true of Char's method in general — that "enlèvement-embellissement" or removing-in-order-to-beautify of which one could be tempted to say too much, thus ruining the point — the details of the original anecdote drop away, leaving only a condensed remainder, all the more forceful for the brevity of its trace.

Compare these lines from the longer, unpublished first version (twenty-three lines in all), called "Flexibilité de l'oubli" ("Flexibility of Forgetfulness"), which include the starting point for the poem quoted above:

> Sans mille bras pour plonger dans les pores
> Tâter le suc de la douleur
> O souvenir aigu des soirs sans riposte
> Sans le claquement d'un adieu
> Chargé à blanc de repentir
>
> Sans l'écumeur de mémoire
> Avide de ce qu'il ne comprend pas
> Vorace de ce qu'il redoute
> . . . .
>
> Boule élastique ce coeur
> Percé de flasques mamelles
> Poches soudées sans espoir de déséquilibre
>
> Les putains aux portes cochères
> Eteignent leurs ombres
> Se lancent leurs linges fumants
> Etoile rose et rose blanche
> Candélâbres en mains les étreignent
> En caresses savantes
> O lèvres inutiles
> . . . .
>
> Without a thousand arms to dive into the pores
> To try the sap of pain
> Oh sharp memory of evenings with no retort
> Without the slam of a farewell
> Loaded with the blanks of repentance

Without the plunderer of memory
Avid for what he does not understand
Voracious for what he fears
. . . .

Elastic ball this heart
Pierced with breasts aslack
Pockets soldered with no hope of unbalance

The whores at gateways
Extinguish their shadows
Hurl at one another their steaming linen
Rose star and white rose
Candlesticks in hand embrace them
With knowing caresses
Oh useless lips
. . . .

As the poem continues, a dead woman's body appears at each ring of the doorbell: all these elements, the picturesque (girls squabbling), the sensual (caresses of meadows, of undergarments), and the sentimental (repentance, farewells, nostalgia in the evening) together with grotesque deformations (the rubber ball and the breasts) disappear to leave only the quintessence of the experience. The presentation, marked as such by the self-reflecting title: "Voici," gives in fact only that which is sufficiently enduring as a résumé of the past moments: the knowing caresses are generalized beyond the grasp of their original donors, and the uselessness now stretches beyond the domain of the lips alone to imply, or so it would appear, the final futility of language itself.

Not just an example of textual condensation, this definitive alteration can also be seen as a model of the poetic and personal development Char manifests throughout his more than fifty years of poetic production. In each period the raw matter of the future text is observed, explored, and condensed.

Artine, a long prose poem on dream, and the densely beautiful prose poems of *Abondance viendra* date from Char's Surrealist period, when he was particularly close to Breton and to Eluard: the language of these poems somewhat resembles in image and tone many poems of other Surrealists, for instance, the violent refusal of commonplace diction, and the will to attack, which characterize even the title *Le Marteau sans maître,* relieved by an occasional lyric gentleness. Furthermore, the crystal transparency of Artine, who is also a river, and all the alchemical themes are familiar to the readers of Surrealism. Char's affection and companionship are deep, once he has chosen his friends, and it cannot have been easy for him to make a formal break with some of his Surrealist companions — but individual conscience and conscious individual work had finally to triumph, for him, over collective production, and commitment even over friendship. In a letter of 1963, he explains: "Because what we were seeking was not discoverable by many, because the life of the mind, a single-strand life, contrary to that of the heart, is only fascinated — in a poetic temptation — by an unapproachable object which shatters in fragments when, having overcome the distance, we are about to grasp it" (*Recherche de la base et du sommet* [*Search for the Base and the Summit*], p. 45).[6]

But the "common" or "shared" presence with other poets and other friends which is described in "Commune présence," the final poem of *Le Marteau sans maître,* makes it clear that the new urgency is highly individual even though the concern is more general:

> Tu es pressé d'écrire
> Comme si tu étais en retard sur la vie
> S'il en est ainsi fais cortège à tes sources
> Hâte-toi
> Hâte-toi de transmettre
> Ta part de merveilleux de rébellion de bienfaisance
> Effectivement tu es en retard sur la vie
> La vie inexprimable
> La seule en fin de compte à laquelle tu acceptes de t'unir
> Celle qui t'est refusée chaque jour par les êtres et par les choses
> Dont tu obtiens péniblement de-ci de-là quelques fragments décharnés
> Au bout de combats sans merci
> . . . .

> > You are in a rush to write
> > As if you were of a slower pace than life
> > If this be so accompany your sources
> > Hasten
> > Hasten to transmit
> > Your portion of wonder rebellion good-will
> > In truth you are behind in life
> > Life inexpressible

The only one you accept at last to join with
Alone refused you every day by beings and by things
Whence you take laboriously here and there a few fleshless fragments
After implacable struggles
. . . .

(MM, 145)

Aware now of his individual task — the neighborly and collective venture of poetry — Char finds even in the center of this common presence, an uncommon singularity: the poet elected both by his peers and by the gods is not unaware of his election.[7] The necessity of writing and of acting, the choice and the moral urgency combined can be said to involve the man as poet whose presence is unique as well as dominant.

Now the first part of the poem "Commune présence" begins with an illumination quite different from the hermetic and alchemical gleam of the earlier poems — included in *Le Marteau sans maître* for example, in *Abondance viendra*. The light is rather open than veiled; in fact, the sun appears as a messenger heralding the coming day: "Eclaireur comme tu surviens tard" ("Light-bearer how late you come"). This poem, with its sense of urgency of a mission felt and accepted, can be seen to play the same role for what we might call the first period of Char's poetic life as does the poem "A***," written in 1953, for another period.

The "common presence" of the title indicates not only the now renewed present of the poet in the world, and the presence of the poet in the text he shares with us, into which the record of his life is intricately interwoven, but again the exterior companionship developing coextensively with the inner experience — as if, in fact, exterior and interior presence were to depend on each other. And yet as the poem ends, the reader is conscious that this common presence is not to be fully shared after all, that there will always remain a part of mystery: "Nul ne décelera votre union" ("None will divulge your union"). Suddenly the question arises as to what other sort of presence Char may have had in mind, what other union, whose outline we are only permitted to glimpse. This very strong sense of withdrawal is constant in Char's work, where reticence finally prevails over self-expression. As he phrases it elsewhere, the poem is the only refuge of privacy for his "too exposed face." Thus a poetry opening onto a space common to all although set apart, closed to any facile gaze, may not reveal the secret "union" of the poet, while nevertheless taking its strength from that union.

II *Shared Presence*

A poet's moral position may often seem to bear little relation to his work. Discussions of commitment, of political attitude are of value only in specific cases and rarely insofar as concerns the text itself. It goes without saying, furthermore, that the critic's own position can unconsciously influence his attitude, try as he may to prevent any leakage between personal belief and professional analysis. From an outsider's point of view, the comments may thus invalidate themselves. For example, Michel Carrouges, a devout Catholic, author of one of the best books on Breton and Surrealism,[8] was finally attacked by the Surrealists for venturing to speak of them before an audience of Catholic intellectuals: his "prejudice" may not seem obvious in his remarks, but the Surrealists' viewpoint is consistent with their theory. In general, I would heartily disagree with the narrow-minded position that would have only churchgoers speak of Claudel, only Marxists speak of Marx, and only practicing Surrealists speak of Surrealism — to say nothing of only French critics writing on French poets. In the writing on René Char, a greater openness than usual is felt. For example in the large volume devoted to him by *Les Cahiers de L'Herne,* the testimonies of his fellow *résistants* in the Vaucluse are found side by side with those of his fellow poets and writers, and an assortment of critics and students of his works, French and non-French,[9] of widely differing attitudes.

Poetics is taken here in its widest sense, that of *poiein,* "to make," so that the working out of a theory should be valid not just for the writing of poems but for living and acting in general. Much the same extension must be applied to all of Char's statements, which are at once directed toward an individual self — privileged because responsible — and a world of unique beings, themselves chosen by the simple choice they have made to read these formulations and to welcome this kind of poetics. Here, poetry is redefined:

Poésie, la vie future à l'intérieur de l'homme requalifié.
Poetry, future life within requalified man.

(SP,10)

In Char's view, a poem is never intended as an ornament to living but is meant to function within its universe. In each successive volume, a few statements on poetry are gathered into a series, so that the definitions accumulate. Elsewhere, we have compared the style of these aphorisms to the *éclats* or flashes of a luminous whole, furnishing an uneven illumination. What is true of the successive groups of aphorisms on poetry we shall be discussing is true of all the series of brief statements making up what we think of as Char's poetics. Of this aphoristic form compared by Jean Starobinski to the Baudelairean *Fusées,* spurts of poetic prose,[10] Char says that it is like a button suited to a buttonhole: if it fits, it fits exactly. Or that it is like an answer to an emptiness, individual each time; and finally, that it is like a tiny morsel of bread hardened in the pocket: it lasts, and it nourishes, if it responds exactly to the hunger one has. Somehow, the aphorisms in general seem to answer needs both poetic and moral; each statement made for poetics holds also for morality, hence the title of the present chapter.

The aesthetic judgments Char makes are usually in favor of a contemporary version of the golden mean, to be more closely identified with perfect measure than with puritanical restraint: he terms the process, as we have already seen, an aesthetic trimming ("enlèvement-embellissement") and compares it to a gardener's task, or to that of a tree pruner. The branch removed permits the others a greater range; the limited number of sprigs on a plant augments their chances. Char's own work, as revealed in his manuscripts, makes this process clear and proves the aesthetic point. When reduced in number from their original profusion, the images lose their possibly "precious" tinge to take on a more necessary character. Writing becomes a moral work also, not merely in its message but in its difficult stylistic being.

The first statement of a consistent poetics appears in *Moulin premier* (*First Mill*), appended to *Le Marteau sans maître,* and so entitled perhaps because it is the first harvest of wheat which must then be processed into flour. It is noticeable that the image includes a human construction, whereas the previous *Premières alluvions* (*First Alluvia*) had not. Here in *Moulin premier,* even if under a different metaphor, the alluvia are gathered up once more, and the harvest yields grains of different sizes and usefulness. Of these, three, which can be extracted and compared, are of particular importance to us and should be considered before moving on to the complete series.

LXIII. We are sure that a poem *functions* when its formula is found to work, and this is so, in spite of the unknown quality of its dependencies.

LXV. That at any demand a poem can efficiently, as a whole as in fragments, throughout its course, *be confirmed,* that is, match its divagations, proves to me its ineffable reality. . . .

LXVI. That at any demand a poem must necessarily *be proved* implies for me the episodic moment of its reality.

So the poem must be seen as coherent: here we think of Char's later statements on the essential order of its parts, whatever their apparent freedom of disposition. Char will call this an "insurgent order." How does the poem express itself — to the outside, or only to the inner vision? The successive statements answer this only half-rhetorical question by successive clarification and differentiation, since poem and poetics must adapt themselves, as surely as the poet himself, to circumstance. "You must be the man of rain and the child of fine weather" (MM, 140). It is a matter of knowing how to adjust.

In fact, *Moulin premier* opens with the lines of a long proselike sentence with the typographical form of verse, on the subject of a "productive knowledge of the Real." There we can discern the inexorable geological ordering of certain eccentric islandlike formations which obscure the voluptuousness of love, and certain skeletons hinting at ancient epochs of species, geographically scattered, which explains the word play on "espaces/espèces." The latter is reminiscent of other word plays such as the "sleep washing the placers" in the poem "Croesus" in the *Poèmes militants* of 1932: the original expression "placer" being at once the ore deposits in a stream (which explains the title figure, Croesus, whom we associate with gold) and the Spanish word for pleasure. Thus sleep is regarded as the bringer of riches and the purifier of carnal pleasures.

The serious point in this opening text is that the knowledge must be collectively satisfying; nevertheless, the text ends with the poet's individual invocation of light as the other member, with him, of a couple to be granted the experience of reality. This opening poem joins immediately with the first paragraph of the prose maxims which follow: "An inhabitant of globes. The childish ambition of the poet is to become a living being of space. Backward from his own destination" (MM, 123). This theme, already present in 1934, becomes, or remains, a major element in the subsequent works, wherein Char will compare himself to a meteor falling to earth, then reabsorbed in the atmosphere as a constellation, of Orion or of Orpheus returned to the heavens: the end of *Le Nu perdu* (*Nakedness Lost*) predicts the Orion poems of *Aromates chasseurs*[11] for its texts are clearly arranged like the stars in that constellation. As a first step in the poetic operation, it is essential to accept, even to welcome, a certain fragmentation without permitting this separation of parts to destroy one's own personality. On the metaphoric level, the operation is clear: the invasion of space must be submitted to, as traditionally, the logical coherence of the personality can be invaded by moments of inspiration, as a considered series of acts can be penetrated by a spontaneous flash. For a visual equivalent, we might consider Hugo's celebrated image of the beggar's cloak riddled with holes, through which the stars shine. That is, against — or through — the fabric black like night, comes an intermittent illumination, all the more precious for its contrast with the obscure. Thus the regular is made valuable by the irregular, the constant by the inconstant, and dark by light, in a reversal of expectation closely related by its tone and its meaning to Mallarmé's themes of shipwreck, constellation, and poem. The image of the cloak with holes becomes rich or diamantine, as absence changes to presence, so that the metaphor of reversal has a material and a moral component. In Char's maxim, to "suffer" or permit an invasion such as that of space is to take an active role in one's own deconstruction and reconstruction, while, on the other hand, it is to oppose one's own destruction. Thus the initially active desire is altered to a passive acceptance before a final return to a strongly active mode with a warning attached. The dialectical development is manifest even in the grammar: ambition de devenir ⟶ subir ⟶ "se démanteler sans se détruire" (ambition to become ⟶ to suffer ⟶ to take oneself apart without destroying oneself).

If I have gone into such lengthy detail over one maxim, unambiguous in appearance, it is for at least two reasons. First, the systematic positive reevaluation of certain functions which might ordinarily be considered negative ones is characteristic of Char's way of seeing; and secondly, as stated above, the theme itself is stressed in Char's future work. A coherent center is implied within these statements in which, as Char points out in the next part of the maxims, "to impose itself all the more, logic takes on the traits of the absurd" (MM, 124).

On the formal level, appropriately, the seventy prose fragments of *Moulin premier* themselves resemble the taking apart of the self, the white of the page dividing the verbal matter into segments; the separate statements show up as black holes on a white page or then as partial illuminations against an emptiness. The reversal is akin to the one already suggested in affinity with the poetry of Mallarmé: a constellation interpreted one way or the other, page and sky, writing and stars.[12] Elsewhere, we read: "La quantité de fragments me déchire" ("The quantity of fragments tears me apart"), and we cannot tell whether the poet or the poem is speaking. In either case this negative is more positive than it might seem.

"L'étincelle dépose" ("The spark deposits"). So reads one of the next fragments. The poet can declare martial law, if he so chooses, electrifying or magnetizing the fields of words, like Breton's and Soupault's *Champs magnétiques* (*Magnetic Fields*), as if sending to battle the warring partners, the opposition of substance and space, gleam and emptiness, the dark of ink and the white of the page, reflection and, most important, intuition, which wins out by arousing all the echoes and resonances possible, giving birth to all the possible forms of poetry. The referential background is particularly dense here, even more so than in the later statements on poetry. The "occult properties of phosphorus" and the opaque waters, the "transfusion of the sun" and the coffin's "fecundation," various male and female images, all these betray the poet's fascination with alchemy, while the image of the phoenix nourished on cinders is related to the traditional fire burning the imagination: "the poet needs more to be 'passionate' than to be taught" (MM, 132).

Even after Char's Surrealist period, he will continue to prize the imagination above all else for its total grasp of what may seem only passing but which nevertheless conveys the eternal, as opposed to pedestrian reason and its prudence: "To the despair of reason, the poet never knows how to 'return home . . .'" (MM, 133). He dwells often in the moment, as if it were an interior place, and the choice of that place over an external one is not without risk, not only of the miscomprehension of others, but also of his own disappointment. For the moment passes also with all other matter into the mill, to be prepared for the eventual nourishment of the poet and of his companions. Thus the image of the "poème pulvérisé," the poem ground into powder for a future utilization.

III *Refusal*

In 1942, Char ("le capitaine Alexandre") was in charge of the Resistance movement in the Basses-Alpes region in southern France. The records and the testimonies of this period reveal the intense courage of the men participating at once in the "furor and mystery" of the epoch, developing throughout a series of experiences often recounted.[13] More significantly for us, the poet's wartime notebook, *Feuillets d'Hypnos,*[14] describes the state of mind as well as of the surrounding universe, interior and exterior conditions. The tone is now and again bitter ("infernal duties"), quietly despairing ("We wander near well-rims from which the wells have been removed" [FM, 110]), and vigorously determined ("Belong to the leap. Don't belong to the banquet, its epilogue" [FM, 138]).

Above all, the uncompromising nature of the man stands out, somewhat in the same vein as Breton's "Haughty Confession": "Absolutely incapable of accepting the fate meted out to me . . . I am careful not to adapt my own existence to the derisive conditions of all existence *here.*"[15] Char's equally firm statements have a double resonance: "I shall write no poem of acquiescence" (FM, 114). The tone carries through to a later text, of a parallel brevity, called "Contrevenir" ("Contravening"): "Nous restons gens d'inclémence" ("We remain men for inclemency.") (LM, 201). Whether it be the inclement weather of the maquis or the vicissitudes of a poet's life lived in large part against the current of the Parisian mainstream, the statement remains a true description of the poet himself: René Char, who claims even now the position of a marginal poet, found in the climate of the Resistance his definitive tone.

The poems of 1938 to 1944, grouped under the title, *Seuls demeurent* (*There Remain Only . . .*) already a title of monumental isolation, show a profound realization of what will from now on be seen as poetic morality. Initially this is developed against the background of a terrible experience suffered through: "On the ridge of our bitterness, the dawn of consciousness advances and lays down its silt" (FM, 19). Spain's tragedy too is part of the bitter acquisition of experience. "Punishment! Punishment!" As the sensibility of a whole generation is developed during these years, so is a companionship based on continuing collective struggle. "I've traveled to exhaustion" (FM, 45), explains Char in "Vivre avec de tels hommes" ("To Live With such Men"), and he speaks not just for his own wartime experience but for what was to come after. Just so, the ending of another prose poem — called by a title which seems to set us at some distance from an understanding of the text: "Ne s'entend pas" ("Unheard") — applies to much of the future work: "No renunciation" (FM, 42). Such a tone chooses to annihilate, for the time it lasts, the line commonly thought to hold between text and life: this is not a literary statement, but rather, a moral declaration.

But the "Refusal Song" which marks the "Début du partisan," or the beginning of a committed personality and action, sketches the outline of what appears to be a retreat from that common presence. "The poet has returned for a long span of years into the naught of the father. Do not call him, all you who love him. . . . He who worked suffering into bread is not visible in his glowing lethargy" (FM, 48). It is impossible to consider the maquis of the Resistance as only a place of political commitment, where necessary action is carried out. How not to see it also as an image of a necessary removal from the too open sight as in the passage already quoted: "You are, poem, the repository of darkness on my too exposed face." Moreover, it forms a parallel to Char's conception of poetry itself. A place committed and yet apart, where action and concealment depend on one another and where the difficulty of the moment seems to strengthen the entire duration of the work: it would be hard to find a better definition of the poem as Char conceives of it. This is a privileged example of the exterior and interior geography to be discussed later.

As the "Refusal Song" ends, a collective performance is once more envisaged, at the instant of liberation: the poet calls again for a "shared presence," stressing the term, lest we take it too lightly as a mere physical manifestation. From now on, creative privacy joins awareness of number; individual refusal and choice reinforce general commitment. The opinions of Char the partisan and of Char the poet are mutually strengthening.

Poetry consists of action, as Rimbaud said: it consists of judgment also, for poetry is neither to be bought nor facilitated. Among Char's comrades, all of them men destined to face inclemency, the poet, like his poem, endures at once "solitary and multiple," keeping his margin about him and yet joining with others. His paradoxical temperament is apparent here as elsewhere, visible in substance and in style: "We are torn between the avidity of knowing and the despair of having known" (FM, 96). Or again, "Wed and do not wed your house" (FM, 94), a statement reminiscent of the tragic poem called "The Swift," the bird who circles about the house and yet is not identified with it, in a flight mediating between the sky's freedom and the inner intimacy. He is felled, like the human heart, for even the least imprisoned among us may be a prisoner to something, if only to doubt: "Doubt is at the origin of all greatness. Historical injustice wears itself out trying not to mention it. That doubt is genius" (FM, 140). But here the poet is careful to distinguish between the genius of doubt and the weakness of uncertainty, which he defines as a wearing away of the senses. Doubt seems to imply for him strength and youth, whereas uncertainty is on the side of the jaded, of that which lingers too long.

And befitting that viewpoint on the importance of time, the best poem will be brief, as are the excerpts in this journal, for practical reasons which luckily coincide with stylistic ones. "I write briefly. I can scarcely *absent myself* for long." Poetry is rapidity of perception — another lesson from Rimbaud — and a complete absence of that paralysis which overtakes the too self-conscious writer. "Poetry is, of all clear waters, the least likely to linger at the reflection of its bridges," we read in *A la santé du serpent* (*Here's to the Snake*). The tone prepares such images as that of the meteor appearing in the "Météore du 13 août" ("Meteor of August 13") and thereafter throughout Char's work. The path of the meteor has a brilliance and an ephemeral quality which makes it an appropriate representation, in its passing, of the poet's own version of his being: "La voie d'or du météore" ("The meteor's golden path") can also be read, by a slight shift, as "la voix d'or" ("the golden voice"). The metaphors are of brightness and speed: "At the second when you appeared my heart had the whole sky to brighten it. It was noon by my poem" (FM, 202). Thus, in *Feuillets d'Hypnos* (*Leaves of Hypnos*), the poet observes, records, and preserves the "infinite faces of the living," all the while protesting against injustice and capitulation. Political attitude and poetics are meant to merge. The stance taken is to be Char's most familiar one: obstinate, concerned, standing against a time of mediocrity.

In this period, *Partage formel* (*Formal Division*) is a deeply optimistic ars poetica ("The poet answers each crumbling of proofs by a volley of future" [FM, 78]), which balances *Feuillets d'Hypnos,* the journal of the embattled poet who writes only briefly, because he does not care to *"absent himself"* for long (FM, 94). In like manner, the inner and the outer works find no definite dividing line but rather a juncture. In René Char's unbending attention to the combined problems of poetics and morality, there dominates, from the beginning, his refusal of an easy renown: to claim a special monumental position because of one's past heroic acts would be as reprehensible as taking a facile road when the other, more arduous, is there for the choosing. The description attached in 1948 to the collection *Fureur et mystère* (*Furor and Mystery*) begins with the words "The poet, as we know, combines lack and excess, goal and past history. Whence the insolvency of his poems. He is in malediction, that is to say, he takes on perpetual and renascent perils, just as surely as he refuses, with his eyes open, what others accept with theirs closed: the profit of being a poet" (RBS, 35). Poems, he continues, cannot exist without provocation, nor poets without watchfulness, both moral and aesthetic. "The poet is the part of a man stubbornly opposed to calculated projects." He may not even consent to a poetic martyrdom, will not die necessarily "on the barricade chosen for him."

The drastic metaphor must not blind us to the real position taken here, lest it be thought that we would situate René Char in one stance, reducing poetic ambiguity. This is a tricky point, and a sensitive one, which bears thinking about. For, reading Char's aphorisms, many of which have a lofty resonance, we might be tempted to consider the poet only in his heroic guise, for instance, in the position of a man tied to his past, filled now with exactly the same fury and searching for exactly the same mystery as formerly, devoted to exactly the same combination of the two: we might thus take the *Fureur* and the *Mystère* to be eternal entities, in eternally lasting proportions. Witness a critic writing on Char's aphoristic style recently: he lamented the poet's attachment to his past at the price of his present.[16] Which is to say that he disregarded — or then found that Char disregarded — the other half of the maxim just quoted about the poet who combines his past with his future goal. We must, of course, permit René Char, insofar as he wishes it, to give the precise weight he chooses to his wartime past. The effect on him was great and the memory has proved ineradicable. Having to abandon all nuance, every shade of hesitation in the face of an actual decision, this necessity changed him forever: "... I want never to forget that I was forced to become — for how long? — a monster of justice and of intolerance, a simplifier, shut off and enclosed, an arctic personage without interest in the fate of anyone who isn't leagued with him to down the dogs of hell" (RBS, 10). But then, afterward, the other seasons replaced that limit-situation, that crisis which, while unforgettable, was not to be resurrected.

"After the conflagration, we believe in effacing its marks, walling up the labyrinth. An exceptional climate cannot be prolonged" (RBS, 15). When Char refused to testify at the trials of war criminals, he proved himself to have mastered that "generosity in spite of oneself" (RBS, 14) that he wanted to acquire. And here he gives us the example of a friend who, the evening after returning from two years in a concentration camp, preferred walking quietly with his dog to denouncing the man who had reported him. This man is plainly one of the few beings the poet would always choose to accompany him, among his multitude of friends, present and absent. And this statement, written as a "Note to Francis Curel," is of such capital importance for Char's moral position — toward poetry as toward life — that we include it in its entirety here. He considers it, in fact, to be "the most complete statement and comment" upon his poetry, and calls it a letter "in which I have defined, at a crucial moment of my existence, my relation to action, to society, and above all, to poetry, a text furthermore addressed to a man who accompanied my youth, and who survived many years in a German concentration camp" (Letter to author, October 23, 1975).

Note to Francis Curel (1958)

In the months which followed the Liberation, I tried to put some order into my ways of seeing and feeling which — against my will — a little blood had spotted, and I strove to separate the ashes from the hearthstone of my heart. Like the Ascian, I sought the shade and reinstated that memory which was anterior to me. Refusal to sit in the Court of Justice, to accuse my fellow man in the daily dialogue as it was resumed, a reaffirmed decision to oppose lucidity to well-being, a natural state to honors, those evil mushrooms proliferating in the crevices of drought and in corners tainted after the first spattering of rain. The man who has known and dealt violent death detests the agony of the prisoner. Better by far a certain depth of earth, fallen in the fray. Action, in its preliminaries and its consequences, had taught me that innocence can, mysteriously, pierce through almost everywhere: innocence deluded, innocence unknowing by definition. I am not holding out these attitudes as exemplary. I was simply afraid of being mistaken. Yesterday's fanatics, those creators of a new type of "continuous murderer," still nauseated me beyond all possibility of punishment. I envisaged only one use for the atomic bomb: eliminating all those, judiciously assembled, who had joined in the exercise of terror, in the application of Nada. Instead, a trial* and a disturbing qualifier in the texts of repression: genocide. You know all this, having lived for two years behind the barbed wire of Linz, imagining all day long your body scattered into dust; on the evening of your return among us, you chose to walk in the fields of your countryside, with your dog at your heels, rather than answer the summons from the magistrate wanting to expose to your sight the excrement who had denounced you. To excuse yourself, you said this strange thing: "Because I am not dead, *he* doesn't exist." In truth, I only know one law which befits the purpose it assigns itself: martial law in the instant of adversity. In spite of your emaciated and other-worldly appearance, you are willing to agree with me. Generosity in spite of oneself, that was our secret wish, measured by the exact timekeeper of our conscience.

There is a meshing of circumstances which must be intercepted at whatever cost: we must practice a cheerless clairvoyance before it becomes the underhanded consequence of impure alliances and compromise. If in 1944 we had, as a general rule, punished rigorously, we would not blush at meeting every day those dishonored beings, ironic wretches not in the slightest discomfited, while a colorless crowd fills the prisons. Someone may object that the nature of the misdeed has changed, since a merely political frontier always lets evil slip by. But we cannot revive the dead whose tortured bodies were reduced to mud. The man shot by the occupant and his helpers will not awaken in the land next to the one where his head was blown to bits. The truth is that compromise with duplicity has been considerably reinforced among the governing class. Those barnacles are laying in provisions. Does the enigma of tomorrow call for so many precautions? We do not think so. But take care lest the pardoned, those who had chosen to side with crime, should become our tormentors once more, thanks to our levity and a culpable oblivion. They would find a way, over time, to slip Hitlerism into a tradition, to make it legitimate, agreeable even!

After the conflagration, we believe in effacing its marks, in walling up the labyrinth. An exceptional climate cannot be prolonged. After the conflagration, we believe in effacing its marks, walling up the labyrinth, and renewing the sense of civic responsibility. The strategists are not in favor of that. The strategists are the scourge of this world, its evil-smelling breath. In order to foresee, to act, and to correct, they need an arsenal which, lined up, would stretch several times around the globe. Prosecuting the past and securing full power for the future are their sole preoccupations. They are the doctors of agony, the boll-weevils of birth and death. They call science of History the warped conscience permitting them to decimate the joy of a forest in order to set up a subtle work camp, projecting the darkness of their chaos as if it were the light of Knowledge. They will new crops of enemies to rise before them, lest their scythe rust and their enterprising intelligence become paralyzed. Deliberately they exaggerate the fault and underestimate the crime. They destroy harmless opinions and replace them with implacable rules. They accuse the mind of their fellow man of sheltering a cancer analogous to the one they harbor in the vanity of their hearts. They are the whitewashers of putrefaction. Such are the strategists who keep watch in the camps and manipulate the mysterious levers of our lives.

The sight of a bunch of little animals demanding the slaughter of a prey they had not hunted, the consuming artifice of a macabre demagogy, the occasional imitation by our men of the enemy's mentality in his comfortable moments, all that led me to reflect. Premeditation was transmitted. Salvation — how precarious! — seemed to lie only in the feeling of supposed good and outdistanced evil. I then moved up a notch in order to mark the distinctions clearly.

For my lack of enthusiasm in vengeance, a sort of warm frenzy was substituted, that of not losing one essential minute, of giving its full value, at once, to the prodigy of human life in all its relativity. Yes, to restore to their natural fall the thousands of streams that refresh men, dissipating their fever. I wandered untiringly on the edges of this belief, I rediscovered little by little the duration of things, I bettered my seasons imperceptibly, I dominated my just gall, I became daily once again.

I did not forget the crushed visage of the martyrs whose look led me to the Dictator and his Council, his outgrowths and their sequel. Always Him, always them, united in their lie and the cadence of their salvoes! Next came some unpardonable wretches whom we should have afflicted in their exile, resolutely, since the shameful luck of the game had smiled at them. Justice invariably loses out, given the conjunction of circumstances.

When a few sectarian spirits proclaim their infallibility, subjugating the greater number and hitching it to their own destiny to perfect the latter, the Pythia is condemned to disappear. Thus do great misfortunes begin. Our tissues scarcely hold. We live on the slope of a mortal inversion, that of matter complicated infinitely to the detriment of a savoir-vivre, or a natural behavior, both monstrously simplified. The wood of the bush contains little heat, and the bush is chopped down. How preferable an active patience would be! Our own role is to have an influence such that the vein of freshness and of fertility may not be turned away from its land toward the definitive abyss. It is not incompatible, in the same instant, to resume one's relation to beauty, to suffer in oneself, and to be struck, to return the blows and to vanish.

One who possesses some human experience, who has chosen to side with the essential, to the extreme, at least once in his life, is occasionally inclined to express himself in terms borrowed from a teaching of legitimate defense and of self-preservation. His diligence, his distrust are relaxed with difficulty, even when his discretion or his own weakness makes him disapprove this unpleasant leaning. Is it known that beyond his fear and his concern, he aspires to an unseemly vacation for his soul? (RBS, 13–18)

*The Nuremberg trials. The extent of the crime renders the crime unthinkable, but its science perceptible. To evaluate it is to admit the hypothesis of the criminal's irresponsibility. Yet *any man,* fortuitously or not, can be hanged. This equality is intolerable. [René Char's footnote.]

So Char returned to peacetime existence, readjusting to a daily cycle, understanding its worth: like the narrator in the prose poem ''L'Inoffensif'' (''The Inoffensive One''), he learned to control his righteous indignation and to accept the turning of the seasons and the change they inevitably bring, as opposed to the one single moment of crisis. Here we think of the harvest poem, "Redonnez-leur..." ("Restore To Them..."), at once a poem of the tragic acceptance of failure and of a sure triumph. "I bettered my seasons": the cycle assures continuity and a profound awareness.

IV   *The Mountain*

Char is, with a few others, one of those who have "chosen the essential, to the extreme..." (RBS, 17). That expression conveys his deepest sense of morality, manifest in his style. Even the terms "essential" and "extreme," chosen rather than some diluting formula such as "in some measure" or "often," reveal Char's absolute and unequivocal, unmodified position. As for the metaphors of morality, he speaks usually of mountains, of climbing and rigor, of the ascent in self-denial necessary to an eventual perspective from the peaks. There is a strong correlation between the elevated sparseness of the setting — the upland bareness so often recurring, particularly in *Le Nu perdu*[17] — and this moral refusal of facile accumulation so that the poor and dry land is made equivalent to a rigorous self-discipline. As the climber divests himself of all his heavy belongings before the final ascent, so the poet is seen to have, or at least to acquire, the nature of an ascetic as well as that of a lover of the earth.

The balance of sparse and abundant, of dry and flowing texts, is quite as marked as that between darker and lighter shades, as, for instance, in *La Nuit talismanique* (*Talismanic Night*), where the talismanic notion suggests no less mystery than the obscurity of night itself, as opposed to, or rather complementary to, the idea of *Les Matinaux* (*The Matinals*) in all its illumination and in its hope of an always new beginning. At last, the moral fervor itself is sufficient to do away with even the metaphors privileged to describe it. Speaking of the volume that includes most of this prose and of its title, which is at the basis of the present discussion — *Recherche de la base et du sommet* (*Search for the Base and the Summit*) — Char explains: "Base and summit, provided that men bestir themselves and diverge, crumble rapidly. But there is the tension of the search...." Now that tension and that search, in their unceasing moral concern, are sensed as the essential elements in the metaphor,

ent as to the ways of grief — the opposite of the furrowed valley of suffering — make up a typical setting in which innocence is threatened and finally defeated. "Mirror of the mureno!/Mirror of yellow fever! Manure of a flat fire held out by the enemy!" (FM, 47). The violence of Char's language is also evident throughout these poems, as in his moral condemnations of an epoch, seen in "Mirage des Aiguilles" ("Mirage of the Peaks"):

They take for clarity the jaundiced laughter of shadows. They weigh in their hands death's remains and exclaim: "This is not for us." No precious viaticum embellishes the mouth of their uncoiled snakes. Their wife betrays them, their children rob them, their friends mock them. They see none of it, through hatred of darkness. Does creation's diamond cast oblique fires? Quickly a decoy to shroud it. They thrust in their oven, they place in the smooth dough of their bread just a small pinch of wheaten despair. They have settled and they prosper in the cradle of a sea where glaciers have been mastered. Be warned. (NP, 17)

The language stands out sharply against that of the lighter poems, for instance, those of *Les Matinaux,* which are traced by only a slight rosy wound, a tinge of suffering, whereas these more violent poems permit no nuance.

The fervent belief in poetry as a moral stance lends a special significance to the tone of Char's poems and to his poetics — whose general outline only we have sketched so far and to which we shall return in the following pages. Few writers have taken greater care to situate their attitude in relation to moral matters: it is perhaps in this care above all that his importance for the majority of readers lies. Char speaks for the poet in general, whose moral purpose we might come to share.

and, as we have seen, Char opts for those elements in
extreme form. Even the metaphor of the mountain p
concern and the extreme choice and reinforces their effe
see its profile rising throughout Char's work, standing
against the sky of the Vaucluse, but also figuratively, in
and in the bareness sought, in the space of a life and

V *Involvement*

"I am concerned about what is accomplished on this ea
laziness of its nights, under its sun we have forsaken" (R
opposed to history, which "ruins our existence with its v
poet chooses the most active contemporaneity. Char in fac
to identify poetry with presence itself. Thus the duty of tl
more human than sublime, more present than transce
"The poet has no mission; on the whole, he has a task. I ha
proposed to build up anything which, once the eupho
passed, was likely to crash" (RBS, 152).

Which is certainly not to say that poetry operates in forge
of the past. Many texts deal with events of the moment
meant to consecrate them to memory: for example, such p
"Par la bouche de l'engoulevent" ("Through the Mouth
Whippoorwill"): "Children who riddled with olives the sun
in the wood of the sea, children, oh wheaten fronds, the fc
turns away from you, from your martyred blood, turns awa
this water too pure, children with eyes of silt, children who
the salt sing in your hearing, how can we resign ourselves
longer being dazzled by your friendship?" (FM, 44). Or aga
poem "L'Eclairage du pénitencier" ("Lighting of the
tentiary" [FM, 46]) or, in particular, "Le Bouge de l'histc
("The Hovel of the Historian"), whose titles are significant i
tion to our discussion about the past and remind us of "l
torienne" in *Le Marteau sans maître*. The latter poem reads in
"The pyramid of martyrs obsesses the earth. . . . Last, in orc
love still more what your hands of former days had only bru
lightly under the olive tree too young" (FM, 47). The effe
many of these poems, where the poet's indignation at injusti
combined with a gentle lyricism, is based on certain recurring
terns such as "water too pure," "olive tree too young": these
ments too extreme, untouched as yet by suffering, therefore in

CHAPTER 2

From Fury to Recollection

I *Matinal Light*

THROUGHOUT the course of Char's work, the poet's personal involvements find their texts, grave or joyous, quiet in tone or more ringing, as reflections of his own moral commitment: they mirror the changing perception of the work undertaken, are determined or depressed, according to the mood of the speaker. Of his Resistance poems — "resistance" taken in all its senses — Char says:

"Il te fut prêté de dire une fois ... les chants matinaux de la rébellion. Métal rallumé sans cesse de ton chagrin, ils me parvenaient humides d'inclémence et d'amour.

Once it was granted to you to recount the matinal songs of rebellion. Metal ceaselessly relit from your sorrow, they came to me damp with inclemency and love. (AC, 43)

As for later "events" — those occurrences supposed to be marked in capital letters in one's life and in one's biography — after 1944 and the end of wartime, their external profile would have to include Char's reactions to the postwar political trials[1] and his praise of the Resistants, his friendship with poets and philosophers and artists,[2] his defense of various positions concerning natural preservation, — all of which are consistent with his general outlook of a "marginal" thinker. As an example in his later years, he has participated in, and led, a movement whose focus was both political and ecological, protesting atomic installations on the plain of Albion in the Vaucluse (see "La Provence Point Oméga") and endeavoring in general to save whatever sites mark a rich heritage.

This is perhaps after all the point: that a poet's protests and involvement count for all of us, that his considered and passionate positions matter for the vigor of their intention, in spite of their local interest and their apparent practical "uselessness." In the long run, the fact that old Catharist sites like Thouzon are vandalized or that trucks can literally carry away the stones forming the old *bories* — those prehistoric stone dwellings found on the land near the poet's home — represents a larger concern.

René Char himself mentions a dividing line in his life at the moment when he was forced to kill another human, becoming "a monster of justice and intolerance, a simplifier . . ." (RBS, 10). The fury of those years is unforgettable, even if the poet refuses all acts of revenge, and it lies unceasingly at the heart of all his perception in the same way as the "absent brother" in the poem of the same name resides like a crucible burning "at the center of unity." Impatience is frequently sensed in the man as in the writing: to what extent it originates in the war experience we would not hazard a guess. But the incontrovertible evidence remains, in the text as in the life: an extreme tenderness alternates with irritation, a tragic and benevolent perception is balanced by anger. The inner outline and the outer continue to correspond.

A. Rougeur des matinaux (Redness of Matinals)

Now Char takes up again the image of the meteor, glimpsed this time in a negative light: "I have fallen from my brilliance . . ." (LM, 81). Or perhaps it is simply that the dawn's redness has subsided. Nevertheless, in spite of such moments (which he refers to elsewhere as the "low cycle"), the characteristics of Char's meteor remain unchanged: first, its intensity with its accompanying mystery. "Intensity is silent. Its image is not. (I am fond of what dazzles me, then accentuates the obscurity inside me)" (LM, 76). Here we think of Tristan Tzara's statement of 1917, in a "Note on Poetry": "Obscurity is productive if it is a light so white and pure that our neighbors are blinded by it."[3] And second, even more important, the uncompromising uniqueness of the passage in which each profile is preserved as distinct from all others: Char warns us again against a too great resembling, grouping our uniqueness with the crowd's similarity: "Wisdom is not to conglomerate, but, in the creation and the nature common to us, to find our number, our reciprocity, our differences, our passage, our truth, and this bit of despair which is its goad and its moving mist" (LM, 76). We might compare the image of the mountain peaks, separate in the morning crimson, with the poet's acerbic statements against a town in which the least folds have been smoothed out, and all citizens conform. In such a "ville sans plis," only a coward would choose to live. (See also the poem "Mirage des aiguilles," in which Char attacks the idea of a civilization free of enigma, where even the snakes lose their mysterious coils.) The meteor — or " the cock's enemy" — remains mysterious; a useful mystery, as Valéry might say.[4]

B. La Bibliothèque est en feu (The Library is Afire)

The poet wills himself sufficiently alone to preserve his space, his freedom, and his *passage:* he should leave traces of his passing, Char says, but no proofs. The insistence on the obscure remains constant. "Free birds do not permit us to observe them," he remarks, and, in another text bearing witness to the same spirit: "Birds do not sing in a bush of questions." Poets leave a margin about them, that demanded by Hölderlin's Empedocles who dismisses Pausanias, by Rimbaud as he "requires everything of us," and even that we take leave of him ("Tu as bien fait de partir, Arthur Rimbaud"; "You did well to leave"), and by Gide, dismissing his reader ("Et maintenant, Nathanaël, jette mon livre"; "And now, Nathaniel, cast my book away"). It is finally of all of us that the poet will require this necessary distance.

From meteor to constellation, the solitariness of the poetic work persists as essential. Here we read a statement which will recur in the series of poetic aphorisms called *Sur la poésie* (*On Poetry*). "The constellation of the Solitary is taut" ([JG], LM, 146). The image of the constellation is that of the poet, singular in his setting and yet collective, an object of general perception and nevertheless unique, solitary like a diamond, or like a star, even when extended against the heavens. We think of the constellation of the hunter Orion as we see it first suggested in the poem "Seuil" ("Threshold") — "I have run to the outcome of this diluvian night. Standing firm in the quavering daybreak, my belt full of seasons...[JG]" (where the belt of Orion might be seen) and then, less obviously, in *La Nuit talismanique.*

The same vision links the poems of the recent *Aromates chasseurs,* where the myth of Orion blinded by Diana (as in Poussin's famous canvas, *Orion aveuglé*) and turned to a constellation, forms the background, and occasionally the foreground, for the entire work. A meteor and the king of the bees, Orion (in "Réception d'Orion'') makes his honey of the earth and then ascends once more to the heavens, so that the myth of blinding and radiance, or descent and ascent, merges with the celestial and mysterious figure of the meteor and the useful animal presence of the bee, whose buzzing is felt here in a poem of the morning, intense and strident like a red color.

Equal attention is given to the actual art of writing. A meditation on the advantages of error, of ambiguity, leads to a eulogy of multiplicity: for the greatest diversity of interpretation depends on an initial imprecision, which poetry will not try to eliminate. And then, on the other side of the paradox, Char insists that his work is one of precision, of the point and the prow: his intricate, often ambiguous, and yet essentially clear poetry confirms this. Once the library of ancient works is set afire, as in the title, we can start over in our recreation of literature, as in our re-reading it.

C. Le Nu perdu (Nakedness Lost)

The first text of poetic aphorisms in this volume opens with space or pause like that suggested in its title "Pause au château cloaque," with another consideration of time, a fascination at the very heart of the volume, which treats returning upland as a temporal climb, in which the past unobtrusively supports us. The determination to throw off useless baggage which might weigh us down for our final climb toward bareness does not entail the absolute exclusion of memory; it only insists on jettisoning a useless nostalgia: "The past would retard the blossoming of the present if our eroded memories did not sleep there ceaselessly. We turn back to one while the other has a fresh spurt of energy before leaping on us" (NP, 22). The climb is clearly marked, even in this pause near the beginning: "Race. First mountain pass: clay weathered away" (NP, 22). Others have been here before, using up the earth, on this rise which is also interior for each of us. We remember Char's frequent descriptions of the poet as mountain climber, to whom there is granted an exceptionally aggressive breathing. The ascent leads finally to the tomb dug in the air, that "dry house" built again, further up, like the dwelling constructed further upstream in "Recours au ruisseau." The profound series called "Lenteur de l'avenir" ("Slowness of the Future") begins with a climb characterized as both mental and physical by its juxtaposition of nouns: "You have to scale many dogmas and a mountain of ice." Next, verbs of triumphant action: "I have demolished the last wall," echoed a few poems later by the definitive motion out of the confines of a dwelling: "Without ceremony, I step across this walled-up world" (NP, 46), and concludes with another statement concerning the three ages of past, present, and future, arranged vertically: "Our terrestrial figure is only the second third of a continuous pursuit, a point, upland" (NP, 38). The climb represented by the *retour amont* is slow, lasting a lifetime. But at the lookout points along the way — these pauses like the "Pause au château cloaque" — the bare upland is seen as illuminated: "amont éclate" ("upland breaks forth"). In his notes to the Italian version of the volume, *Ritorno sopramonte,* Vittorio Sereni comments that a reddish brightness is always seen above the peaks toward which the movement leads. He reminds us of Char's expression: "un brisant de rougeur" ("a breaker of redness"), a presence of light which is, in fact, felt throughout the darkest of visions.

The climb which the poetry represents is not intended only for the poet alone, and not only for one season; it takes place, no matter what the conditions ("we remain men for inclemency"): *"Where shall we spend our days* at present?... *Let us stay in the quarried rain and join to it our breathing"* (NP, 51). The aggressive respiration of the mountain climber joins the animal breathing of those continually exposed to downpour, snow, and sun: *"we shall hold together under the storm become forever familiar"* (NP, 51). Sereni points out a passage in which the poet identifies himself with the plant and animal life in answer to the alienation of contemporary affections. "Aliénés" begins: "From the shadow where we were..." (NP, 110). Thus in the following poem whose title we have already commented upon, "Buveuse" ("Drinker"), the plant absorbing endless water is allied also to the poet who has been discouraged with the devastation of nature by the warlike installations of men: "why should we still liberate the words of the future of the self now that every speech soaring upward is the mouth of a yammering rocket, now that the heart of every breathing thing is a stinking cascade?" (NP, 53).

In "Le Terme épars" ("The Scattered Term"), each of whose flashes is brief or sparse, Char reminds himself, and us, of our commitment to generosity and forgiving, on this upward path which is also that of the mind: "Give always more than you can take back. And forget. Such is the sacred path" (NP, 55). "The evening frees itself from the hammer, man stays chained to his heart'' (NP, 55). Compare another text from *Le Nu perdu:* "Generosity is a facile prey. Nothing is more frequently attacked, confused, defamed. Generosity creates our future executioners, our retrenchments, dreams written in chalk, but also the warmth which receives once and gives twice'' (NP, 91). The text ends on a streak of red light in the distance, representing the future, a silence free from our present doubt and misgivings as they are tied to our words: "How uncurious truth would be bloodless if there were not this breaker of redness in the distance where the doubt and the saying of the present are not engraved. We advance, abandoning all speech in promising ourselves that sight'' (NP, 56). The profound silence is, like the space the poet demands about him, a denial of everyday triviality at the final height. Significantly, the next series of *fusées* has to do with both silence and motion: "we would have only liked to answer mute questions, preparations for movement'' (NP, 58). In the title the poet includes Maurice Blanchot, a well-known critic whose advocacy of silence and the poetic mystery are closely associated with Char's own. Char speaks for them both, then, in this ascent at once temporal, spatial, and moral: "The time is near where only that which could remain unexplained will be able to summon us'' (NP, 58). That ideal bareness we cannot really recreate is akin to silence and to mystery: all three converge in the poetry and the "irresolute and misunderstood infinite'' which is said to surround it (NP, 58).

As we look in succession at the texts of *Le Nu perdu,* the distance up the mountain seems measured out like the "Tide Ratio'' of *Les Matinaux;* here the flux is no longer only that of water, but also of space and time. From the "Pause'' and the "Slowness' we arrive at the "Tables of Longevity,'' where we read, still in relation to the infinite, a future couched in a present tense: "When there is less and less space between the infinite and us, between the libertarian sun and the prosecutor sun, we are aground on night'' ([JG] NP, 61). But it is some time before the "bell of pure departure'' will signal the triumphant end of the battle upland: "True victories are only won over a long time, our forehead against the night'' (NP, 65). The struggle is again that of upstream as well as upland and is openly marked as being so. A beautiful series of aphorisms called "La Scie rêveuse'' ("The Dreaming Saw'') moves from an initial line of understatement and blossoming ("To be sure of one's own murmurs and to lead action as far as its word in flower'') through an invocation to the river to whose modest murmur we were listening (''Law of the river . . . , of losses compensated but of torn sides, when the ambitious house of the mind crumbled, we recognized you and found you good'' (NP, 69) to the final statement of persistence in spite of difficulty, toward the recapturing of a true identity (''Alone among the stones, the stone of the torrent has the reverie-like contour of the face finally restored'') (NP, 70).

This text comes from the collection *Dans la Pluie giboyeuse* (*In the Quarried Rain*), from whose heavy and nourishing fall the torrent was created, to whose animal intensity the poet hunter or the poet as his own prey has joined his breathing and his fate: that hunter who is associated with the flower called Orion's dart, with the unicorn in ''L'anneau de la licorne'' (''Ring of the Unicorn''), as well as the poem ''Seuil'' (''Threshold''), as we have seen, will later appear in a ''mute game,'' then at last in his own constellation before redescending to earth in *Aromates chasseurs* as Orion Iroquois. The path upland leads through all the texts, for in the constellation glimpsed within the poem ''Possessions extérieures'' (''Exterior Possessions'') traces of many myths might be seen to merge, for example, Orion the hunter, changed to a dove, a bee, and then a star, and Orion blinded — as in Poussin's canvas *Orion aveuglé,* already mentioned, which telescopes two legends[5] — but by his own radiance. The blinding or the self-blinding ray resembles the single horn of the animal in ''The Ring of the Unicorn,'' in *La Nuit talismanique.* Here Orion, not named but no less present, chews a leaf of a virgin flower, a hunter never satisfied with his prey: ''He had felt jostled and lonely at the border of his constellation, only a little town shivering in tempered space. To the questioner: 'Have you finally met her? Are you happy at last?' he did not deign to reply, and tore a leaf of guelder-rose'' (NT, 83). But this Orion remains as tragic as he is lucid; ''The more he understands, the more he suffers. The more he knows, the more he is torn. But his lucidity has the measure of his pain and his tenacity, that of his despair'' (NP, 89).

Orion will reappear, assuming in himself all the rising of a return upland and the falling of a meteor, all the scattered brilliance of *La Parole en archipel* (*The Word as Archipelago*) and the clustered radiance of his own constellation, bridging the heavens and the earthly streams for both senses of the return upland, human as well as mythic. To the path of the return, a mystery is still assigned. "The roads which do not promise the country of their destination are the roads most loved" (NP, 91). Upland in all its bareness must remain open to interpretation; it will never be reduced to one landscape, neither that of the Vaucluse nor that of the heavens. Similarly, to join the figure of Orion, already the convergence of so much legend and of so many myths, there now comes another hero, Hölderlin's *Hyperion* — "The best son of the old solar disk and the nearest to his celestial slowness" (NP, 95).[6] Hölderlin himself, stricken with madness by the gods as if by a lightning bolt, and thus singled out as a poet, is a chosen figure of René Char. Heidegger's essay on Hölderlin ("Hölderlin and the Essence of Poetry") comes close to the spirit of Char's poetics, as do many of Heidegger's writings, with their emphasis on being-toward-death and its relation to being-in-this world. (Some of Char's most moving prose has to do with his friendship with Heidegger, which can be called poetic as well as philosophic.)

The breaker of redness has now become a crepuscular light, itself said to be bare like older times, magnified like a torrent swollen with rain, and as peremptory as the lightning which apparently chooses the poet. These terms are used by Char to describe his night of fire, resembling Pascal's terrible night to whose brief, jagged, and unforgettable "mémorial" Char's most intense passages now bear such a strong likeness.[7] These texts have about them a suddenness and yet a gravity which set them apart. The very violence of that night marks the culmination of the path upward toward what is no longer a simple line of daybreak, magnetic in its attraction, but a passionate light of conflict, where even the word *brisant* becomes active rather than descriptive, changing from a noun ("the breaker") to a verb: "se brisant de toutes ses artères contre nous" ("breaking with all its arteries against us") (NP, 97).

That passionate vision prepares a quieter illumination. After the breaking down of walls and the scaling of heights, the poet goes once more inside, having acknowledged all along that the path of returning was interior, as the summit is finally an invisible one: "I have lived outside, exposed to all sorts of inclemencies. The hour has come for me to return, oh laughter of slate! into a book or into death" (NP, 106).

II *Outlook: Recherche de la base et du sommet*
      (Search for the Base and the Summit)

Often, as we know, a poet's theory is most clearly seen in his essays on other writers or artists — more clearly, indeed, than in his essays centering on his own poetics. Char's recently published volume of commentary on the major artists whose world he values — *Le Monde de l'art n'est pas le monde du pardon* (*The World of Art is not the World of Pardon*) — shows a range of writings from diverse epochs and concerning equally diverse creations. His comments, for instance, on Georges de La Tour, Miró, Braque, de Staël, Vieira da Silva, as well as on Baudelaire, Rimbaud, and Nietzsche, together with his conversations with Heidegger and his remarks on Camus, indicate the ways and depth of his thought. Even the intonation can prepare us for Char's own poetry. For instance, in describing Miró's achievement, Char finds the evocative phrase: "the taste of springs and of their flight," (RBS, 83), a formulation applicable to many of his own poems. The elements of water and air, the motions of beginning and soaring, the suggestion of an entire cycle — all are complete in that one line. Miró, says Char, indicates, without spelling out or proclaiming: that is also a good description of the essential concern characteristic of his own work in the graver moments. "We recognize the painter's gesture by that gravitation toward the sources which, as they appear, turn the images aside from their end. As if breathed in by the movement seizing them, they contract" (RBS, 83). The description might well be that of the intense expectation and occasional massing of Char's own images, under the sometimes hidden weight of an idea, felt to press even on the movement of the poem itself.

Or a passage on Nicolas de Staël, which by chance serves as a useful reference point for Char's own play on the abominable snowman. Char, in discussing the illustrations of de Staël for some of his poems, writes that they "appear for the first time on a field of virgin snow that the sunlight... will try to melt" (RBS, 93). De Staël and he are not, he says, abominable snowmen, "but we sometimes come nearer to the unknown than is permissible, and to the empire of stars." Like that of Char, de Staël's art is the contrary of long-winded; it is rather, like his, of a lapidary simplicity and shows a natural ellipsis. Of all the artists with whom Char has been allied, de Staël seems — to this reader — the closest to him, along with Braque.

Concerning theory, the latter seems of the closest temperament:[8] we have only to read their conversations, as Char relates them here, or to consider the similar humanity of their characters. Indisputably, André Breton's writings on and his admiration of Picasso or Matta reveal Breton's way of thinking as nothing else can, for instance, Breton's essays in *Le Surréalisme et la peinture* on Picasso's venture across the abyss or on his juxtaposing of objects, and on Matta's reshaping the entire universe to fit his own vision and to make way for chance. Just so, Char's writings on Braque further our understanding of the poet as much as of the artist. To take an example corresponding to the one just related from Breton and Picasso, Char says of Braque the following: "Children and geniuses know that there is no bridge, only the water allowing itself to be crossed. Thus in Braque's work the spring is inseparable from the rock, the fruit from the soil, the cloud from its fate..." (RBS, 57–58).

Char describes in his work the "incessant going and coming from solitude to being and from being to solitude": this sure convergence of the natural, the human, and the universal on one hand and of this alteration from the one being to the being-in-the-world is constant in Char's writing. We have only to think of his essay on the artist Sima, in which he discusses the junction of the four elements and the situation of man-in-the-world: "I am not separated; I am among" (*Se Rencontrer paysage avec Joseph Sima*).[9] Braque knows how to "judge an enigma, how to revive for us its fortune and its benumbed brilliance" ("son éclat engourdi") (RBS, 67). When the poet despairs, as in the phrase already quoted: "Je suis tombé de mon éclat...," the artist, above all others, can render to him his inspiration. For he symbolizes continuity: Braque's work of one day, maintains Char, if it were to be suspended over the abyss in the evening, would carry over like a projection toward the morrow's work. Char finally likens these germs of the next day's work — "a multiplier in the expectation of its multiplicand" (RBS, 87) — to a threatened candle which the sun would soon replace. In *La Nuit talismanique,* the poet warns us not to substitute for the flickering chiaroscuro of candlelight, its flame rich in imaginative possibilities and ambiguities (that "éclat nourri de sa flamme"), the steady brightness of day.[10]

Braque, like Char, "recreates his candle" every evening, never sacrificing the indispensable mystery in favor of what is at best only clear. The candle in several of La Tour's canvases around which the other masses are grouped,[11] makes a fitting image for an observation as quiet as the flame: "Action is blind, it is poetry that sees." Similarly, we might observe the lighting in Char's major poems as an example of poetic interiority. These two kinds of light serve to nourish one another, like Breton's image of the communicating vessels of day and night; for Char, poetry and action will be the interdependent "vases communicants." So the contemplation of the flame and the daytime motion ("Emerge on your surface...," RBS, 168) are joined.

Among the philosophers whose poetics are close to Char's own, Heraclitus seems one of the nearest. The fragments which have survived from his writing are like poems, each chosen by chance to endure above all that has been submerged. For Char, convinced that our only certainty for the future is an ultimate pessimism ("the accomplished form of the secret where we come to refresh ourselves, to renew our watchfulness and to sleep," RBS, 117), Heraclitus represents a solar eagle. He is a profound predecessor, and an uncompromising one: "He knew that truth was noble and that the image revealing it is tragedy." Likewise, Char's own poetry is not sad; it is exhilarating, complicated, forceful, and often tragic.

Two other poets — for Heraclitus is, for Char, as much a poet as a philosopher — lend a psychological strength and a nourishing unrest to his language: Baudelaire and Nietzsche are Char's "water-carriers," sources of his poetry and of his disquiet. He defines poetry now as "the wound that shines where the sentence effaces itself" (RBS, 139) and finds Nietzsche's "seismic anguish" close to his own.

Rimbaud is a significant predecessor as many critics have pointed out. "But if I knew what Rimbaud meant for me, I would know what poetry is before me, and I would no longer have to write it..." (RBS, 130). One of Char's numerous commentaries on Rimbaud indicates sufficiently his particular importance: "we must consider Rimbaud in the single perspective of poetry. Is that so scandalous? His work and his life are thus revealed to be of an unequaled coherence, neither because of, nor in spite of, their originality.... We are fully aware, outside of poetry, that between our foot and the stone it weighs upon, between our gaze and the field traversed, the world is null. Real life ... is only found in the body of poetry" (RBS, 127). Poetry has, for Rimbaud, for Char, possibly for all true poets, no other reason for being than being. Rimbaud's famous statement quoted by Char is infinitely applicable to the latter's own poetry: "I meant to say what it says, literally and in all senses" (RBS, 127).[12] Rimbaud was, like Char, a lover of nature, seen as a luminous force, joining with the language of the poem for a lasting creation. His spirit pervades Char's notion of the three ages, recurring in the title of *Le Nu perdu* and in a text of *Aromates chasseurs,* which are, respectively, the story of simplicity and unfeigned spiritual nakedness — that is, the golden age — as they are lost in an industrial age, and that of a middle time we must find again, by retaining the value of the past and predicting the future. "Rimbaud escaping[13] locates his golden age in the past and in the future. He does not settle down. He has another epoch come forth, either in the mode of nostalgia or in that of desire, only in order to fell it instantly and to return to the present, that target with the *center* always hungry for projectiles, that natural port for all departures." This spatial description of past and future and present serves to map the three ages, already mentioned; Rimbaud's rhythm, many of his conceptions, and his dynamics are Char's also: "In the motion of an ultrarapid dialectic, so perfect it does not arouse *panic,* but rather a whirlwind, fitting and precise, he pulls us along, he dominates us, carrying everything with him ... as we consent" (RBS, 131). Not only is there to be no settling down in comfort for poetry, but no permanent attachment to what we have most loved: "The urgency of his word and its scope espouse and blanket a surface that language before him had never attained nor occupied." In fact, Rimbaud is perhaps best known, in Char's works, for his uncompromising departure, to which we have already referred. Char defines poetry as "the song of departure": how, he asks, could such a poet as Rimbaud have been satisfied with less than complete separation? For "poetry is the distanceless solitude among everyone's bustling, that is, a solitude which has the means of expressing itself." Our aloneness, even our loneliness should be as refreshing for us as the fountain nourishing the brutality of a poet: "To drink shivering, to be brutal, restores" (NP, 82).

III   *Night and Reflection*

The volumes now to be discussed are turned towards an inner

realm: towards a "talismanic night," a gathering of reflections about the deepest aspects of poetry, and, finally, a constellation.

A. La Nuit talismanique (Talismanic Night)

These texts are each a witness to solitude and to a contemplation both cosmic and minute. Some add or strengthen aspects which we had not clearly seen before: for instance, concerning the importance of the small and the minimal, less as a plea for modesty than as an insistence on our *perception* and on our reordering of values. In line with this attitude, Char praises the man who takes care of his working instruments, in full knowledge of their value. We must assign the proper place to things and gather about us all we might use, in time of drought. (The importance of water in the austere landscape of the Vaucluse can hardly be overstated: thus the chosen images of scarcity and aridity.) This volume is turned toward the interior, as a kind of challenge to the mind. Since no movement in Char's work is entirely simple, there will be an extension outward subsequent to this introspective stage: "The night brings nourishment, the sun refines the nourished part" (NT, 15). Just so, this talismanic night provides the temporary halt and the renewing source for later works.

Again we hear the plea for space to be created about the poet: "The obligation, without pausing to breathe, to rarify, to hierarchize beings and things intruding on us" (NT, 72). The mutilated giant who will finally take on the traits of Orion is subject to laws outside himself over which he has no intellectual command, but here he controls the space of his own contemplation, choosing its light and "inventing" his own sleep. He concentrates on the flickering of one candle, on its circular dance, triumphing over the partitioning of days (as in the "divided" time or "cloisons" of an earlier poem, "Faction du muet"): "As night asserted itself, my first task was to destroy the calendar viper knot where the start of each day sprang to sight. The aboutface of a candleflame prevented me. From it I learned to stoop over and to straighten quickly in the constant line of the horizon bordering my land, to see, nearing, a shadow giving birth to a shadow through the slant of a luminous shaft, and to scrutinize it" (NT, 87). The text is called "Éclore en hiver" ("To Blossom in Winter"), and the deepest meditation in its inward flowering is encouraged by just this close scrutiny of a minimal event, requiring careful attention.

One of the more interesting lights to cast on this volume is a light
of difference, in a comparison of these texts with the brief opaque
splendor of Mallarmé's *Igitur,* built around the expectation of one
gesture, the breath which will extinguish a candle at midnight. The
consequence of that annihilation of being by the breath is ambig-
uously positive: the creation of shadow and the union of word and
act. For here the breath which has served in speech serves then as
destruction; the observation is of especial interest for us, in view of
the wide scope and extraordinary frequency of the images of
breathing in Char's writing, from the earliest volumes. The complex awareness of certain extremes ("the presence of Midnight,"
the absolute presence of things) and of absolute emptiness (a
"vacant sonority," "reciprocal nothingness") is echoed by another
violent contrast shared in the common space of the two poets. The
poles of dark ("shadows disappeared in obscurity") and of a
flame, of chance and necessity, of ancestral apparitions hanging
over the quiet yet lucid meditation of an open book on a table surrounded by mystery, all these find their place within the shadows of
Char's talismanic night.[14] Both texts depend on a temporary sus-
pension of breath before the candle is extinguished, with the extinc-
tion of the text as its necessary corollary. Even the old gods storm-
ing outside the room where the poet plagued by insomnia keeps
watch over the candle and the page remind us of Mallarmé's "dieux
antiques." It is as if René Char had assembled his writing and
drawing instruments on the table where Igitur's book is open, in a
space no less haunted by presences: "Another hand protects the
oval flame," and the presence is as mysterious as that other presence of midnight. "The heart of night was not to be set afire. The
obscure should have been the master where the dawn's dew is chis-
eled" (NT, 16). Valéry points out "The usefulness of mystery."
"The best work is the one that keeps its secret longest."[15]

The volume bears witness to the "desert sand" of insomnia,
where the waters of night nourish like the redemption by water in
"Le Visage nuptial" ("The Nuptial Countenance"). Igitur closes
the book and blows out the candle "with his breath that contained
chance," while the poet stands fast in his nocturnal quiet, until the
daybreak described earlier in the poem "Seuil," where the figure of
Orion may be seen to make his appearance against the horizon. Yet
that interior meditation retains the hospitality of the hearth:

J'ai couru jusqu'à l'issue de cette nuit diluvienne. Planté dans le flageolant petit jour, ma ceinture pleine de saisons, je vous attends, ô mes amis qui allez venir. Déjà je vous devine derrière la noirceur de l'horizon. Mon être ne tarit pas de voeux pour vos maisons. Et mon bâton de cyprès rit de tout son coeur pour vous.

I have run to the outcome of this diluvian night. Taking my stand in the trembling dawn, with my belt full of seasons, I am waiting for you, my friends who will come. Already I divine you behind the black of the horizon. My hearth's good wishes for your homes never dry up. And my cypress walking-stick laughs with its whole heart for you. ([JG] FM, 181)

Char's nocturnal meditation accommodates all of the landscape outside, taking within its range harvest, sun, the wind of the mistral, the river, and the land beyond. From the candle he watches, this "sedentary flame" itself containing the household gods propitious to our contemplation, he moves to an observation of the stars, of the human sky as it is matched to the universe beyond man. Thus the talisman, whether held by the poet's hand or that of another, serves as a guide to whatever is beyond the contemplation of any one night or any series of texts with its single or multiple source.

B. Sur la poésie (On Poetry)

In *Sur la poésie* Char collects several previous statements on poetics written between 1936 and 1974. The statements will be referred to according to their proper order, so as not to falsify the evolution once chosen, which is then reexamined by the poet in his reprinting of these texts. They begin by an echo of *Moulin premier:* "I admit that intuition reasons and gives orders from the moment that, as a bearer of keys, it does not forget to set the embryonic forms of poetry in motion, crossing through the high cages where the echoes are sleeping, those elect precursors of miracle which, as the forms pass by, steel and fecundate them" (SP, 71). As in the text *En trente-trois morceaux* (*In Thirty-three Pieces*), the fragments chosen and reassembled, taking on a different order, find a new coherence; the definitions of poetry itself may appear differently lit in this rereading of poetry as the realized "love of desire remaining desire" or as the future life of "requalified man." Now the previous image of wool strands extended ("laines prolongées") joins with that of a spiderweb on the same page, form replying to like form, as well as with the other images of making and of long enduring, through a dialectic of presence and passing: "The vitality of the poet is not a vitality of the beyond but an *actual* diamantine point of transcendent presence and pilgrim storms" (SP, 13).

And this dialectic is balanced by another, that of the torment and the happiness of the poet as they are always intransitive, the poet drawing "unhappiness from his own abyss" (SP, 17). It is important here to make a distinction between the writer in general and the poet in particular, for Char's morality and poetics are specifically fitted to the "métier du poète," his chosen location in space and time to the "logement du poète," his passion for life to the "vitalité du poète." For example, the following statements do not start, and could never have done so, in Char's universe, with the words "Être écrivain" ("To be a writer"), but rather, with the words "Être poète." Near the outset Char reconsiders the poet's own place ("The poet cannot remain for a long time in the stratosphere of the Word") (SP, 8) and his mission ("The poet, keeper of the infinite faces of the living") (SP, 9). "To be a poet is to have an appetite for an unease whose consummation, among the whirlwinds of the totality of things existent and intimated, provokes happiness just at the moment of conclusion" (SP, 13). The poetic function actively liberates, at its source, the only wealth found valuable: the verb *tourmenter* carries perfectly in both languages the double sense of a creative disturbance strong enough to arouse and of an inspiration sufficient to realize all that was only potential. In short, it indicates a *troubling activity,* both positive and negative: "The poet torments with the help of immeasurable secrets the form and the voice of his fountains" (SP, 14). It will be noticed that even the source is individual, not general.

Above all, these statements manifest a vivid faith in continuity, even when the poet leaves whatever he might consider as the base of his too prosaic safety for the risk implied in this conception of the poetic. He does not choose to remain untouched by his involvements: "Lean over, lean over more," he reminds himself — and us (SP, 15). Typically, rather than merely speaking the "truth," he maintains that he must live it (SP, 19). Now he takes advantage of the miraculous enduring of the smallest things, like the poor man profiting from an olive's eternity, as he phrases it elsewhere. Or again, at every disappointment in the expected — for in a "profession of risk," nothing can really be counted on but the certainty of that risk — this "magician of insecurity" (SP, 18) responds with a confidence whose foundation is often far from evident to us, and all the more affecting: "To each crumbling of proofs, the poet replies by a salvo of futures." And later: "Poetry will steal my death from me" (SP, 20).

The situation of the mind turned-toward-the-future is closely allied to the metaphors of climbing toward a height from which the poet, called a "summit of breath in the unknown" (SP, 16), can see forward and around at a great distance, leaving behind him the feats already accomplished of which he is no longer a simple reflection. He is no longer to be compared to others since he fits neither their norms nor their hopes, neither is he tied down to possessions. He thus occupies a perfect position for superior or future action. "The serene town, the unperforated village is before him" (SP, 16). The statements surrounding this one are noticeably full of increase and of upward growth. Everywhere the relation of the exterior or the physical to the moral and mental is clear, as in our chapter title "exterior and interior architecture." The text directly following the one just quoted begins with a simultaneous description of the poem and of its poet: "Standing erect, increasing throughout its course, the poem..." (SP, 17). The initiator of verbal action is also the arranger, not of a placid still life, but of an "insurgent order" which is inscribed in the future,[15] rebellious to past tranquillity and even to past truth. "You cannot begin a poem without a parcel of error about yourself and the world..." (SP, 21). So the spirit of contradiction or at least of ambivalence remains. Many of Char's more profound statements are structured along those lines: for example, "poetry is the fruit we hold, ripened, joyously in our hand, at the same moment it appears to us on the frosted stem, within the flower's chalice, of an uncertain future" (SP, 21). Living amid truth makes one a liar, claims Char (SP, 19), and exactly that spirit of ambivalence and dialectic moves us beyond individual pettiness and pride to a certain impersonality. There is, however, no coldness to the term, rather a feeling like that in the poem "The Extravagant One," in which a frost grazes the surface of the wanderer's forehead, "without seeming *personal*" (FM, 182).

The perception of contrasts is often a matter of outlook and of patience in examining detail: "... il est permis enfin de rapprocher les choses de soi avec une libre minutie..." ("...we are finally permitted to bring objects near us with a free exactness...") (*En trente-trois morceaux,* April 8, 1956).

By a paradoxical twist, just as the aphoristic generalizations which we discuss here under the heading of morality may seem to have a particular application, so the observation of the smallest objects, the juxtaposition of which composes the universe of Char's daily observation, may appear to find the widest scope. To give only one example of the rapid expansion of perspective, let us take, in *La Nuit talismanique,* the line: "Fourche couchée, perfection de la mélancolie" ("Pitchfork laid down, perfection in melancholy"). The eye, and with it the mind, travels from the object to its announced position, to the representation of the mood or its emotional effect, and then to an implicit question as to situation. Why the halt? Will the work halted continue? The answer is, in all probability, positive, and the reason, temporal: "Successives enveloppes! Du corps levant au jour désintégré, ... nous restons constamment encerclés, avec l'énergie de rompre" ("Wrappings, one after the other! From the rising body to the day disintegrated ... we remain constantly surrounded, with the energy to break off") (NT, 65). The phenomenon is somewhat reminiscent of Pascal's celebrated statement on the meeting of extremes: Char's contrasting wide and narrow focus are equally important for our understanding of his overall perspective. We might compare this stretching of the imagination to other mental exercises: first to one of Char's own observations on vertical extremes, already quoted, applicable to these roughly horizontal extremes of focus: "Base and summit ... crumble rapidly. But there is the tension of the search...." Here the value is placed on an effort surely as much moral as physical, in this "Recherche de la base et du sommet." The ability to take in the distance between two extreme points and to juxtapose them nevertheless, to grasp the complex relation between them, all that is essential for poetic understanding. Moreover, we might see in the extraordinary proliferation of all varieties of contrasts the same mental athletics required of the reader, if he would follow the work with any fidelity.

Now the balance of opposing terms requires a movement between the components of the individual statements which can properly be called dialectic, in that the statement itself serves as the final term. In turn, a series of statements can be seen as moments in the temporal advance toward an integral statement on poetry, necessary movements in themselves, whose individually contradictory and yet eventually resolved terms accumulate in a balance sensed as delicate and complete.

We saw above an example of the relation of one moment to the next, where a description of the poet as the "summit of breath in the unknown," whose being cannot be tied down or measured, led to the expression: "Standing erect, increasing throughout its course..." by way of the metaphors of height and increase, and an earlier example, where the "prolonged wool strands" into which the poet transforms each potentially dying object led to the image of a spiderweb hung in the sky — or with its concentric circles reaching from line to line. Such relations can often be traced through a few moments in succession, each adding to the preceding information without altering its own dialectical progress. For example, a series of three statements on death makes up a whole, evidently related to other statements and yet still sufficient unto itself. Each statement shows its own obvious exterior and interior contradiction and subsequently, its own more subtle resolution; it should be noted, parenthetically, that we are still following Char's own order for these aphorisms, so that the sequence of discussion is first of all controlled by his arrangement of texts.

To make a poem is to take possession of a nuptial beyond, which is found well within this life, closely attached to it and nevertheless in near proximity to the urns of death.

*   *   *

Poetry, unique ascension of men, which the sun of the dead cannot obscure in the perfect and burlesque infinite, perfected and ludicrous.

*   *   *

Poetry is at once speech and the silent, desperate provocation of our being, exigent as it is ("être-exigeant") for the advent of a reality which will be without rival. It is incorruptible — imperishable, no, for it is exposed to common dangers. But the only one which visibly triumphs over material death. (SP, 24–25)

The moments are not only joined together in theme — what conquers death and gives value to life? — but also, in form. The construction is strong, or, to use a musical description, the opening attack is vigorous. The set of three terms is joined to the subsequent fragment by implication of the death theme: "The only signature at the bottom of the blank sheet of life is traced by poetry" (SP, 26), and to the preceding parts by such definitions as the following: "Poems are incorruptible bits of existence which we hurl toward death's repugnant muzzle, but high enough so that, ricocheting onto it, they fall into the nominative world of unity" (SP, 22). (This concept is closely related to Heideggerian thought.)

Since poetry is necessarily a situation of disquiet, value attaches not to calm but to unrest, to the rebellious intellect, "refractory to calculated projects." For, "Poetry lives on perpetual insomnia" (SP, 26). The contradictory attitude itself corresponds perfectly to that state of unease and nonprogression which it magnifies. It is genuinely an exciting venture: not a pseudoheroic escapade, but rather one to be taken seriously, or not attempted at all. "In poetry, you only dwell in the place you leave, you only create the work you are detached from, you only obtain duration by destroying time" (SP, 28). Again, on the next page: "The act of writing, poignant and profound when anguish raises itself on one elbow to observe and when our happiness thrusts itself uncovered into the wind of the path" (SP, 29). The play of one concept against another, while it allows both stability and flexibility, prevents stagnation.

In the most recent part of the book, some previously unpublished statements are gathered under the dedication: *A Faulx contente* (*To Your Scythe's Content*). We think, in reading this title, of the opposite melancholy of the pitchfork laid to rest at evening in *La Nuit talismanique.* The image of the scythe serves as a metonymy for the ideal of pruning and trimming, for the sacrifice of what is unessential; it is therefore, unlike the pitchfork, not laid to rest.

We are still following a marked path along *Sur la poésie,* that of the contradictory and finally resolved terms of much of Char's writing, exemplified in another image of anguish: a path chosen by the poet leads, he says, only "to one's own bloodied heart, the source and the sepulcher of the poem" (SP, 33). Above all, the point of a poem, its beginning and end, is *not* exterior representation, which Char would associate with prose. The poet is of a sensitivity such that the extremes touch within each text, occasionally far inside: sometimes his writing expresses a quiet ambivalence, sometimes the clash of opposing forces. The next to the last statement reads: "the poem lays us in a postponed grief, making no distinction between the cold and the ardent" (SP, 34). The adjectival terms even in their opposition show a slight unbalance, for we would expect either frigid/ardent or cold/hot. But "ardent" is precisely the term which matters here, for a multiplicity of reasons. A poem is, for Char, ardor expressed or suggested, intuition at its highest point; yet it is at the same time the product of a clear-headed and rational process; it thus represents emotional weight and imaginative spirit.

The complexities and ambivalencies of the opposing terms are seen with some of their prolongations in the final statement of the volume, where the role of the poet now assumes the functions of freeing and joining: "The poet bursts the bonds imprisoning what he touches; he does not teach the end of linking," reads the last statement in the book (SP, 35). The linking of element to element can be perceived in a form identical with the essential and traditional double nature of all profound relationships. The relations of poetic elements will not be simple, and therefore continue despite the conclusion of each poem, or of each series of statements, each slight imbalance encouraging the extension of thought.

From each twist of the "prolonged strand" of the poet's thought, there comes another possible one, joining a literal to a figurative, a physical to an emotional term. The same bifurcation can be seen in many words: for an example, the French word *source* has an extension far beyond its English usage, as seen in the double definition: "source and sepulcher of the poem." For the source is equally the liquid origin and the inspirational *spring,* at once figurative and geographic, moral and actual. Thus the specific word "source" renews itself, in one more prolongation, by its own ambivalence, through all the endless links a poem creates. We read, in a retrospective extension from "A Faulx contente," the title of the poem "La Faux relevée ("Scythe Lifted Again"): "Fontaine, qui tremblez dans votre étroit réduit,/Mon gain, aux soifs des champs, vous le prodiguerez" ("Fountain, trembling within your narrow nook,/My gain you'll spread bounteous to fields athirst") (LM, 184), as if this were also a source, a spring of poetic ambivalence and abundance, of poetic enduring, in correspondence with the poetics which always underlies it. Finally, all Char's meditations, whether on aesthetic or moral matters, could be entitled: *Sur la poésie.*

C. Aromates Chasseurs (Aromatics Hunters)

These poems follow an inward path, made up of meditations on political and moral problems, on poetry and survival in the present world, and yet the path remains in direct and strongly sensed correspondence with one constellation in the sky, that of Orion. The

volume takes up and expands the brief texts from *Le Nu perdu* on
the relation between poet and destiny, expressed by the image of
stars against blackness, with the play of bright and dark fully as
complex as that of Baroque poetry. The architecture, with its
columns leading from earth to sky — four corresponding texts of
Orion — will be referred to again in the chapter on "The Elements
of the Poem," since each has its own element. This architecture
seems particularly close to that of Mallarmé.

The four great Orion poems which form the pillars of the volume
are inserted in the constellation, at once the archipelago from
which Orion descends because of a thirst for earth in the initial
poem, "Evadé d'archipel" ("Escaped from the Archipelago"), and
the sky to which he finally returns, garbed in an "infinity" of
luminous points. They are set in the series of radiant islands as a
structure — visible and implied — to whose light each bears a brief
witness. The volume itself joins all the elements, as the aromatic
smoke returns the hero to his heaven, to build there the giant pon-
toon bridges under which we can pass safely, after our swim "in the
icy waters" connected to the earth. Orion Iroquois, a builder in
steel and at great heights, is the figure corresponding to the hunter
Orion blinded and received on high ("Réception d'Orion"), these
two figures forming the two central pillars or columns of the book,
the first and last poems of Part II. Just so, the first and last poems
of the volume correspond, for in "Evadé d'archipel," Orion has
put down his arrow and his sickle, and in his meteoric fall, his traits
are blackened with crude celestial ore, like those of the laborer in
the early poem "Fréquence" or those of the maquisards in the
Resistance poems, all in *Fureur et mystère*. And the last poem,
"Eloquence d'Orion," will answer this one, by its own resistance
songs: "les chants matinaux de la rébellion. Métal rallumé sans
cesse de ton chagrin, ils me parvenaient humides d'inclémence et
d'amour" ("matinal songs of rebellion. Metal relit ceaselessly from
your pain, they came to me damp with inclemency and with love")
(AC, 43). The suffering and the fire are implicit, merged with the
morally unforgiving nature: we remember the earlier refrain: "We
remain men for inclemency" from "Contrevenir." In this last
moment of eloquence, Orion would choose to be, in all simplicity,
by a river and in a poem, before his departure:

Tu t'établirais dans ta page, sur les bords d'un ruisseau, comme l'ambre gris sur le varech échoué; puis, la nuit monté, tu t'éloignerais des habitants insatisfaits, pour un oubli servant d'étoile. Tu n'entendrais plus geindre tes souliers entrouverts.

You would settle in your page, on the bank of a river, like ambergris on the seaweed adrift; then when night had risen, you would depart from the unsatisfied inhabitants for a forgetfulness serving as a star. You would no longer hear your half-open shoes complaining. (AC, 43)

CHAPTER 3

Exterior and Interior Architecture

I *Relations*

THE following discussion is based on the supposition that the particularly noticeable images in the works of a given period can be analyzed together as an informal system of signs, indications of the probable attitude of the poet at that moment. The very approximate nature of the observations is to be stressed, since — as in Proust's analyses of love — germs of a later development are likely to be present within any work or any experience which is in turn never free from certain traces of former attitudes. Granted that any schema is rough, it is still possible to sketch a changing configuration from the early works to the later, accepting the problems and paradoxes entailed in such an effort.

The nature of a specific text may often be clarified by contrasting it with another: thus, for example, the hard metallic imagery of *Le Marteau sans maître*. Its extensive series of alchemical images, its architecture of castles and fortifications, and the sort of living creatures found there will not occur again in Char's work. A definite change is felt, from the heavily fortified atmosphere of the former to the sensitive world of the later work such as *Les Matinaux* or *La Nuit talismanique*; the very kind of animal present in *Le Marteau sans maître* is in accord with the harshness of the other images, in this early volume, with its enigmatic surface.

II *First Scene*

To begin with, let us examine this configuration of the early works in more detail, under the aspects already suggested, those of animals and of metals, before turning to the outer geography of the landscape and the inner configuration of the text which reflects it.

58

In résumé, the metallic images are often related either to fire (to be discussed in the following chapter: "The Elements of the Poem") or to intensity, such as the violence of a revolver, an image combining both: "the knot of metal which deals death." As the title might indicate, the *Poèmes militants* (*Militant Poems*) of 1932 are dense with this kind of image. One poem (MM, 81) opens with a vaguely alchemical allusion: "Celle qui coule l'or à travers la corne" ("She who runs the gold through the horn") and concludes with a stanza in which first the metallic glow is integrated with the animal kingdom, via the image of the phoenix, reborn from the flame, and then contrasted with a dull and neutral background: "Dans un ciel d'indifférence/L'oiseau rouge des métaux/Vole soucieux d'embellir l'existence" ("In a sky of indifference flies/The red bird of metals/Concerned to beautify existence"). Then the entire experience is threatened with silence and dispersion after that intensity of flame and concern, and this new atmosphere is closely related to the "indifference" of the sky and pervaded with uselessness: "La mémoire de l'amour regagne silencieusement sa place/Parmi les poussières" ("The memory of love takes its place once more, silently/Among the dusts"). This poem, entitled "L'Historienne," is a microcosm of the world represented in *Le Marteau sans maître,* not only in its alchemical and metallic substances, but also by the stress it lays upon the active and the vigorous elements:

> Nous qui ne confondons pas les actes à vivre et
>   les actes vécus
> Qui ne savons pas désirer en priant
> Obtenir en simulant
> Qui voyons la nuit au défaut de l'épaule de la dormeuse
> Le jour dans l'épanouissement du plaisir

> We who do not confuse the acts to be lived and
>   the acts lived-out
> Who do not know how to desire by praying
> To obtain by pretending
> Who see the night in the joint of a sleeping woman's shoulder
> The day in the blossoming of pleasure
>
> (MM, 81–82)

Two other sets of images are intimately linked to this stern moral attitude, heavily represented in this collection. First, the image of the bird: as we suggested in the preliminary remarks on harsh images, the birds in these poems show mainly a predatory or a vainglorious nature. Thus the eagle, appearing "on the mountain" (MM, 19) or on watch in "La Luxure" ("Lust"), one of the militant poems, is not without menace: "L'Aigle voit de plus en plus s'effacer les pistes de la mémoire gelée/L'étendue de solitude rend à peine visible la proie filante" ("The eagle sees the tracks of frozen memory effaced more and more completely/The stretch of solitude renders scarcely visible the prey streaking by") (MM, 67). Like the memory of love taking its place once more amid the ruins in the poem discussed above, even this frozen memory fades away so that only the animal strength remains.

The other most striking animal image is again linked to superiority and display of that distinction. Among the early poems of *Arsenal* (1927–1929) the one called "Tréma de l'émondeur" ("Diaresis of the Pruner") reads, in its entirety: "Parce que le soleil faisait le paon sur le mur/Au lieu de voyager à dos d'arbre" ("Because the sun spread out its peacock tail on the wall/Instead of traveling on a tree's back") (MM, 20). Because . . . then what? The implicit answer to our question is perhaps very simple: then . . . this poem itself, like its own enigma and solution, each referring to the other unendingly. The poem, when it was originally printed as one of the seven in *Le Tombeau des secrets* (*The Tomb of Secrets*) (1930) was called "L'Exhibitionniste." In a sense, all the poems of this volume are exhibitionistic poems, full of energy displayed and resonant in tone, most of their images stressing a dominant vitality.

"Robustes méteores" ends with a revolutionary statement, like a call to arms: "Levez-vous bêtes à égorger/A gagner le soleil" ("Rise up beasts to slaughter/To win the sun") (MM, 21). Those beasts are certainly not tame ones, nor is the panther who stalks the pages of *Moulin premier* any less menacing in attitude. Whether it be involuntary or calculated on the part of the poet — for the debate as to that issue will never be satisfactorily resolved — the choice of these specific kinds of animal is, like the choice of what might be seen as stage sets or props for the poems, significant. Everywhere a deep and vibrant red color seems to prevail: openly in the "roulotte rouge au bord du clou" ("the red caravan on the edge of the nail") (MM, 57), by implication in the forge and anvil (the latter prow-shaped as if for departure: "les nacelles de l'enclume" ("the skiffs of the anvil") (MM, 56), horrendous in the vivid crimson of the flayed ox whose tongue and whose cry penetrate the most striking of the prose poems of *Abondance viendra* (1933), a sickly purple in the "ultraviolet castle atop a town laid waste by typhus" (MM, 115), as well as in this red bird of metal passing like a phoenix through the flame and in all the other fiery images within the long series of alchemical images. In this volume, the white of a chalk exhausting itself against a black slate (in a poem ironically entitled "Intégration") and the black magnifying glass, "arcane currency forgotten by the repulsive savior," in "Eaux-mères" — a geological term, a place name, and permitting of several different phonetic readings — contrast with the red images in a verbal tricolor whose cloth is unfolded as a background for the present verbal abundance, suggesting another poetic abundance, which will come.

The architectural framework remains to be pointed out in this brief sketch; it is prepared by the first texts of *Arsenal,* as if the entire volume were to be situated in an armory for the easy storage of weapons, in view of a future need. Nor is the image of the armory a unique projection of the critic. Repeated mention is made of a "fortress," of a "château fort" with its moat (MM, 22), its battlements (MM, 29), and its dungeon (MM, 20). The veranda (MM, 22), the woods (MM, 20, 28), and the hothouses (MM, 41) are not out of keeping with the fortified domain (as in the title of one of the texts in *Abondance viendra:* "Domaine"). There is often a strong sense of place in Char's writing, a definiteness of setting in many of the poems as a deliberate relief from the lofty abstraction characteristic of the moral aphorisms. Much of his poetry is firmly *located.*

Now the hothouses remain in his poetry until, in 1938, they form part of the scene of the epic love poem *Le Visage nuptial* (*The Nuptial Countenance*): "Je ne verrai pas les empuses te succéder dans ta serre" ("I shall not see the mantis replace you in your greenhouse") (FM, 60), just as the prisons and ruins (MM, 59) remain present during the war years. These enclosed spaces will gradually diminish later, in favor of the open, the free, and the mountainous landscape. The "roulotte rouge," the horse-drawn carriage, and the racetrack of *Artine* vanish in Char's later writings, as the apartment laid with saltpeter in the same text makes way for the inner and more metaphysical room for meditation of *La Nuit talismanique,* where the whole scene shifts to the interior; but the one

major image of the "pure eyes in the woods," in their endless
search, remains, showing clearly the need for a mental dwelling
beyond the architectural particularities of any exterior setting.

In *Le Marteau sans maître,* the furnishings of the texts are simple
indeed: beds and tables, with the former particularly prominent in
the early poems. For example, in this volume alone there is the bed
described at the beginning of *Artine,* in which a large number of
objects from the animal, mineral, and natural kingdoms are
thrown together: a small bleeding animal, a lead pipe, a gust of
wind, an icy seashell, and so on, as if the bed were the perfect Surrealist meeting place for divergent objects — the equivalent both of
Lautréamont's dissection table, where an umbrella and a sewing
machine meet, and of Breton's fruit bowl, where he wanted to see,
not a pear alongside an apple, but something of a different order,
which would stretch the mind and enlarge the imagination. In a
poem entitled "Les Messagers de la poésie frénétique" ("The
Messengers of Frenetic Poetry") (MM, 58), suns are said to
descend medieval rivers and to sleep in the crevices of rocks, "on a
bed of. shavings and of gnarls," a natural resting place. A young
girl's bed appears later in another poem on poetry, "Le Climat de
chasse ou l'accomplissement de la poésie" ("The Hunting Climate
or the Accomplishment of Poetry") (MM, 63). In "Chaîne," which
could be considered by its title to be relevant to the making of
poetry itself and to the forcible convergence of elements in it, the
bed is taken as a gathering place as well as a final resting place, as in
the later poem from *Le Nu perdu:* "J'ai reconnu dans un rocher la
mort fuguée et mensurable, le lit ouvert de ses petits comparses
sous la retraite d'un figuier ... Sans redite, allégé de la peur des
hommes, je creuse dans l'air ma tombe et mon retour" ("I have
recognized, in a rock, death fugal and measurable, the open bed of
its small assistants under the seclusion of a fig tree ... Without
repetition, freed from fear of men, I dig in the air my grave and my
return") ([JG] NP, 20). In the early poem on hunting, the bed is
linked with death, but nevertheless leads the way to light, in a progression partially indicated by the title already expressing a perception of linking — "Chaîne":

> Le grand bûcher des alliances
> Sous le spiral ciel d'échec
> . . . .

Des lits de mort sous les écorces
Dans les profondeurs vacantes de la terre
. . . .

Sur la paille des fatalistes
L'écume d'astre coule tout allumée
Il n'y a pas d'absence irremplaçable.

The great funeral-pyre of joinings
Under the spiral failure sky
. . . .

Death beds beneath tree bark
In earth's vacant depths
. . . .

On the straw of fatalists
The foam of stars flows fully lit
There is no absence irreplaceable.

(MM, 71)

Here we might notice, in passing, the play of dark against light which follows the model of many earlier poems, for instance: "La chute des torrents dans l'opacité des tombeaux/Les sueurs et les malaises annonciateurs du feu central" ("The torrents falling into the tombs' opacity/The sweats and unease announcing the central fire") (MM, 67–68).

In the poem, a "failure sky," a rotted boat, and "death beds" pave the way for the rising images of "new wings," for "radiant effort," and for the luminous foam of constellations. And in fact much of the volume is constructed in that fashion: the schoolyard is afflicted by the malady of meningitis, and the prisons, tombs, hot-houses, all the accumulations of ruins, dust, and the shards of bottles not only signal the negative side of experience, the downfall and degradation of what was once entire, but also prophesy violent change. The "catastrophic stone" found in one of these poems is, while fraught with menace, illumined by the prediction of alchemical alteration, like a Rosetta stone, as if to reveal the secret language of metamorphosis. And in fact, many of the subsequent uses of the bed image can be related to its association with the crucible, both serving to mingle opposing elements for a future transformation — the bed figures often in alchemical works as the locus of the *conjunctio oppositorum* ("conjunction of opposites"): male and female elements, fire and water, earth and air — those elements making up the theme of a later chapter in this book. In the double image of the "arnica au soleil et le lit au matin," (MM, 84), for instance, yellow flowers and bruises are equally present, so that the sun, in its destructive, flowering, and heat-giving functions, comparable with those of a crucible, is juxtaposed with the bed.

In the overall scope of the work, many of the images reflect this one, or are at least relevant to it: the hothouse with its fermentation of possibilities, the prow of the boat linked with the forge ("nacelles de l'enclume") — thus, the convergence of adventure and preparation as of implicit water and implicit fire — and even the other vehicles such as the rotted boat, the red caravan, the "washed and renovated horse-drawn chariot" of *Artine* — these vehicles in every case are to be preferred to the "saltpeter-papered" apartment where Artine's enemies are to be entertained. Of course, in a sense every tomb, every prison (and there are many here) and every schoolyard, infected or not with meningitis, are images of that bed and crucible, as an enclosed or prepared place where one is necessarily available for adventure, sufficiently withdrawn from the ordinary space of things to accomplish an extraordinary act.

The bed/crucible identification as a central focus for the poems in *Le Marteau sans maître* finds its perfect scene in the architecture of which we have the composite picture in various poems of this volume: a fortified, crenellated castle with a moat, a castle whose outline in an almost lurid "ultraviolet" stands atop a hill above a devastated town. In the dungeon or in the cellar of the castle, an alembic is set up, an image to which all the subsequent images of the forge are clearly related, and which corresponds to a coffin. Over this castle there stretches a "roof of sorrow," and in its drafty reaches, various "vacillating" elements find their unsteady place: doors, corridors, various nooks and crannies of the trapdoor and cellar-window variety: "soupiraux, réduits."

In the light of this present reading, therefore, the negative line formerly traced along the path of certain images of decomposition, putrefaction, and disintegration can be reevaluated positively. The long list of elements corresponding to that line of downfall: dust, decomposition, rotting, ashes, effraction, leprosy, specks of ashes, opaque waters, and so on, will be recuperated in a dialectical recovery: "l'homme criblé de lésions par les infiltrations/ . . . /les massifs du dénouement" ("man riddled with lesions from infiltra-

"the sky of the stream" (LM, 61), or in "Eprouvante simplicité"
("A Trying Simplicity"): "Mon lit est un torrent aux plages des-
séchées. Nulle fougère n'y cherche sa patrie" ("My bed is a torrent
with dried-up banks. No fern looks for its country there") (NT,
86). In "L'Extravagant" (FM, 82), the bed is avoided during the
hours of sleep, but otherwise, used for dreaming, as white birds
pass over the ceiling. It becomes the very image of death in the
poem of circumstance, "Le Loriot" ("The Oriole"), written on the
third of September, 1939, its three lines sufficient to convey the
despair of the period: "Le loriot entra dans la capitale de
l'aube./L'épée de son chant ferma le lit triste./Tout à jamais prit
fin" ("The oriole entered the capital of dawn./The sword of his
song closed the sad bed./Everything forever ended") (FM, 33).

But often a sense of death seems to accompany the image: in "Le
Mortel partenaire" ("The Mortal Partner"), a death-love struggle
takes place on a white surface, at once a bed and a boxing ring. In
"Devancier," air, rock, and a fig tree form the poet's tomb and his
final return, the latter suggested in several poems, one of which is
set by the oceanside, where the face of death and the words of love
are said to merge: "la couche d'une plage sans fin avec des vagues y
précipitant des galets — sans fin" ("the bed of an endless beach
with waves throwing pebbles on it — endlessly") (NP, 80). Another
is set in a garden, but a metaphysical one, where a couple are seen
to struggle bodily in a brutality confessed to be refreshing, and still
another, in a field of wheat, where two daggers protect: "pour
garde et pour viatique" ("for a guard and for viaticum"), the lark,
because it alights, and the raven, "the spirit which engraves itself"
(NP, 83). Again the bed is only present in suggestion. In these last
several examples, the resting place seems final, giving no hint of an
alchemical resurrection.

On the other hand, the table, not noticeably present in the early
poems, appears more and more frequently, as the image of generosity and community spirit, easily shared by all: "Heal the bread.
Bring the wine to the table." ("Attabler le vin.") In the play *Le
Soleil des eaux,* the meal shared by Apollon and Marie-Thérèse, is
plainly rich with generosity and love. The elements in Char's work,
as in his life, do not lose their simplest reality through any symbolic
significance beyond themselves. As opposed to the hidden sickness
of contemporary society suggested by many of Char's observations, the significance of this table and those bearing similar repasts

tions/ . . . /the mountain chains of the resolution") (MM, 87).
the alchemical process each element must be initially degraded i
its negative aspect for the final reconstruction to take place:

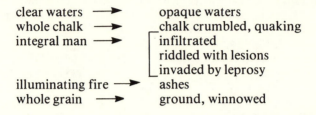

clear waters   ⟶   opaque waters
whole chalk   ⟶   chalk crumbled, quaking
integral man   ⟶
       infiltrated
       riddled with lesions
       invaded by leprosy
illuminating fire   ⟶   ashes
whole grain   ⟶   ground, winnowed

Then the elements are reconstituted in an alchemical or a m
phoric transformation. The bed becomes the riverbed for the br
body of water flowing through the prairies in "Eaux-Mères,"
the transforming quality the Surrealists always ascribed to w
has its chance to take full effect. This purification and clarificat
in turn leads us to the poem "Crésus," in which the gold *placer*
the river Pactole — according to legend full of those deposits
may be washed from the stream, or then, from the poem.

No less than the moral of the harvest, the teaching of alchem
taken as real and as cyclical: for the Work is never completed
must always be done again. All the images of reconstruction
finally grouped in an interior architecture by the reader, accord
to the recognizable signs showing through the apparent obscu
and apparently hermetic conglomeration of these poems, th
selves forged on the "nacelles de l'enclume," whose images f
nevertheless uninterruptedly one into another like those of Elua
Poésie ininterrompue.[1]

III   *Table, Lamp, and Fruit*

Sometimes the tracing of one element can aid in the perceptio
an entire development. The elaborate architectural setting and
interior scenes of *Le Marteau sans maître* are replaced in the l
poems usually by the simplest of indications — the castle is
placed by a river, a mountain, a path, or a garden. The image of
bed remains but seems to lose its alchemical reference, becom
simply the bed of a stream in "Recours au ruisseau" ("Recours
the Stream"), where, mingled with the reflection in it, it beco

cannot be overlooked. Like the garden, it displays its offerings guilelessly. Such frequent images as the fruit bowl, brilliantly illuminated by the summer light, and in which opposing elements can meet, are the natural equivalent of the alchemical crucible, merging and transmuting, in a heat just as real as it is metaphoric. (Of course, the fruit is already a token of exchange, as in some ancient marriage rites: see, in our *Presence of René Char,* the pages on fruit in Char, Hölderlin, and Heidegger, and see also Char's poem "Les Lichens," in which the narrator asks "true night" to use his own sleep to give happiness to the woman he loves, concluding: "Et tous les fruits t'appartiendraient" ("And all the fruits would be yours") (LM, 64).

Again here the emphasis is on the genuine or the natural entity as opposed to what is artificially cultivated and sophisticated; thus the "nuit véritable," in granting his request, grants also the plenitude of fruits. Now in Char's image of the fruit bowl, the container and the contained demonstrate often the same relation as in Breton's "compotier," which contains, ideally, elements from different categories — that is, a concretization of Reverdy's initial advice on the taking of two opposed objects from widely distant fields so that illumination can take place. (Breton suggests, for instance, that a pear should not be called upon automatically to take its place beside an apple, but that a crab might occasionally do so, in order that the limits of perception be stretched, the not-already-thought replacing the what-has-been-thought-too-often. So he turns the work and the word, together with the imagination, toward the future.) The exterior illumination is thus replaced by an interior one, which extends further and deeper below the surface. In Char's "burning fruit bowl of summer," found in *Contre une maison sèche* and whose unity is in some way the reflection of the unity of Char's entire work, the illumination does indeed seem to come from the inside as well as the outside, to be occasioned in part by the very disparity of what the otherwise neutral container contains. (Nor is this necessarily a perception of summer: "Affermi par la bonté d'un fruit hivernal, je rentrai le feu dans la maison" ("Strengthened by the goodness of a winter fruit, I carried the fire into the house") (NP, 46).

In any case — even apart from the real and metaphoric value of what is offered upon it — the table with a bowl of fruit is characteristic of the tone of some of Char's poetry, resembling some of Braque's canvases, those of Fernandez, and other like painters. It was in homage to Fernandez that the poem "Rémanence" was first published. In this text, all the past hospitality comes to shadow the present suffering: "De quoi souffres-tu? . . . Comme si, la haute lampe et son éclat abaissés sur une assiette aveugle, tu soulevais vers ta gorge serrée la table ancienne avec ses fruits" ("From what do you suffer? . . . As if, the high lamp and its radiance inclined over a blind plate, you were to lift toward your anguished throat the old table with its fruits") (NP, 76). The lamplight fills the room, penetrated here by a nameless and unspecified pain: the expanse of the table accommodates many feelings other than those of generosity and fulfillment.[2] The nostalgia is poignant, and the question posed is answered at the end by an abstraction closely linked to the image of nourishment, spiritual and material, only half-utilized: "From the unreal intact in the reality laid waste" . . . From that which was chosen and left untouched . . ." (NP, 76). Contrast this with the utter tranquillity of the meal in "L'Amoureuse en secret" ("Loving in Secret"), whose scene closely resembles, except with more subtlety, the meal of *Le Soleil des eaux:* the food, the light, and the love are woven together in a delicate narrative fabric whose surface is unbroken:

Elle a mis le couvert et mené à la perfection ce à quoi son amour assis en face d'elle parlera bas tout à l'heure, en la dévisageant. Cette nourriture semblable à l'anche d'un hautbois.

Sous la table, ses chevilles nues caressent à présent la chaleur du bien-aimé. . . . Le rayon de la lampe emmêle, tisse sa distraction sensuelle.

Un lit, très loin, sait-elle, patiente et tremble dans l'exil des draps odorants, comme un lac de montagne qui ne sera jamais abandonné.

She has set the table and brought to perfection what her love seated across from her will speak to softly in a moment, looking hard at her. This food like the reed of an oboe.

Under the table, her bare ankles now caress the warmth of the one she loves. . . . The lamp's beams tangle, weaving her sensual distraction.

She knows a bed, far off, awaits and trembles in the exile of sweet-smelling sheets, like a mountain lake never to be abandoned. (LM, 57)

The lamplight shining on the table here has no anguish about it; rather it intensifies the calm assurance as even the bed in its "trembling" seen through the woman's eyes conveys a unique tone of fidelity and future continuity, matching the simple perfection of the surface, the nourishment, and the implicit resonance of the oboe. (It might be said, at least parenthetically, that, whereas the place of music in Char's work is less apparent than the place of the visual arts, to which so many texts bear witness, his texts are as remarkable for their vibrations and the resonance carrying from one to another as for their visual aspect.)

Char's room can be as simple as the room which appears so often in the poems of Reverdy: a lamp, a table, a hand, a face ... Whereas in Reverdy's room a mirror or a painting, a wall or a window, places a limit on the space, for Char, the room usually seems limitless, precisely because the light focuses on the desk, or on the table, with no physical extension beyond; therefore the inner and mental extension is potentially endless. The prop of any scene and the objects of any poem are generally determined by the feeling; Reverdy's space is lonely, the figures are distant one from the other, as we would expect, whereas Char's figures are sometimes alone, but often joined in feeling and in action, real or metaphoric.

The worktable of the poet is most explicitly in sight in the volume where the external architecture is evidently lacking, in *La Nuit talismanique*. Here the space of the mind absorbs all other details, as the lamp hanging over the table in the two poems just considered, "L'Amoureuse en secret" and "Rémanence," is now replaced by a flickering candle which would have been appropriate neither to the anguish of the one nor to the quiet sensuality of the other but which perfectly fits the night of dreaming and signs. In retrospect, we might feel that all Char's poems were written at that same table, with that same idea of a talisman as a guide, from the alchemical and aesthetic experimentation to the wartime meditation and action, from the rage to the mystery, from the clear poems of *Les Matinaux* to the poems of night and rain, such as *Dehors la nuit est gouvernée* (*Outside the Night· is Ruled*) and *Dans la Pluie giboyeuse,* from the early abundance to the opposite pole of bareness, to *Le Nu perdu* and this other and profound talismanic night.

IV *Geography and Structure*

Divorced entirely from its content, seen at first glance, the geography of this universe differs greatly from volume to volume. *Les*

Cloches sur le coeur (*Bells on the Heart*), *Le Tombeau des secrets,* and the poems of *Le Marteau sans maître* are devoid of proper names. The landscape could not be localized and the texts, with the sole exception of the alchemical imagery of *Abondance viendra,* are more captivating in their tone than in their specific imagery. The flexible intertwining of images and the cumulative resonance attached to certain figures develops through the successive volumes, until the density of reference is enormous within this single universe, extending beyond its apparent and exterior scope to an interior one.

In brief, *Le Marteau sans maître* is devoid of visible specific geographical allusions, and this is largely true up to the moment of the wartime poetry. There the poem and the name converge, with a few adventures visible on the exterior and others only implied. Occasionally, titles of places or events mark the moments to be stressed, as in the wartime journal, *Feuillets d'Hypnos,* which abounds in implied details. "La-France-des-Cavernes" reads one subtitle; the poet speaks of "Florence who was returning to the Moulin de Calavon" and of "Olivier le Noir" who was asking for water to clean his revolver. We are permitted to see the figures as clearly as we see the reproduction of Georges de La Tour's painting *Le Prisonnier* in the room where the poet is working.

Among the superb poems of *Le Poème pulvérisé,* the "Hymne à voix basse" ("Hymn in a Low Voice") (FM, 177) begins with an invocation to the Hellades as the source of a "breeze of knowledge and the magnetism of intelligence," nourishing, not only for Greece, but for us all, a series of forces which are at once tied to a soil in its specific fertility and perpetual as they are universal, "this massive soil made up of the diamond of light and of snow, this land which cannot spoil under the feet of its people, victorious over death, but mortal by the evidence of its purity..." (FM, 177). The poem was written at the time of an exhibition for the Greece of the Resistance,[3] as Char informs us in his commentary on this group of poems.

The eloquence has nothing vague about it: "Oh Greece, mirror and body thrice martyred, to imagine you is to restore you" (FM, 177). Another of these poems, "Donnerbach Mühle," written in the winter of 1939, begins with a clear picture and an equally clear sound, to which the repeated verb "entendre" draws attention:

> Novembre de brumes, entends sous le bois la
> cloche du dernier sentier franchir le soir et
> disparaître.
> . . . .
>
> Glas d'un monde trop aimé, j'entends les monstres
> qui piétinent sur une terre sans sourire.
>
> November of mists, hear in the woods how the
> bell of the last path crosses the evening and
> disappears.
> . . . .
>
> Death knell of a world too well loved, I
> hear the monsters who trample over the
> unsmiling land.

> (FM, 175)

These are poems which "let themselves be interrogated," since the poet comments on each of them later, in the *Arrière-Histoire du poème pulvérisé* (*The Background of the Pulverized Poem*). But in any case, their profile is characteristic of the later volumes, a mixture of the closed and the open, of the geographically definite and the poetically implied.

Of course, the greatest writing transcends its original moment and its place of origin to acquire universal importance. As we have pointed out at some length elsewhere,[4] this poetry is anchored in the Vaucluse but spreads out to a universal space and to a moment beyond Char's own, as beyond ours. It is nevertheless true that to know his country is to know not only the exterior landscape as a setting for Char's thought but also a certain determination of its tone and temper. The light there is, in fact, unlike the light elsewhere, and the shadows on the Mount Ventoux shift from purple to green in a quite singular way; the very dryness of the land makes an inescapable contrast with the fountains which enter so often into the poetry. This play of the sparse and the dry against the abundance of the water's flow and surge, as well as that of the piercing light against the shifting shadows, offers its own contrast as a scene for the highly marked relief of the writing. And yet a reader who had never seen the Vaucluse and its dry rocks, who had no acquaintance at all with the illumination and the colors of Provence, might perhaps suppose such a backdrop for the poetry itself. But the

poetry greatly enriches the landscape for those readers who contemplate it, whether for the first time, or in a continuing famil-
iarity.

Now the landscape of the Vaucluse, whether actually seen or only
sensed through the poems, seems intimately connected to a moral
attitude as well as to an aesthetic one. For to the sparseness of the
vegetation and to the special dryness of the heat there corresponds,
as has already been stated, a refusal of the easy in favor of the more
difficult (RBS, 13), a positive identification of man's natural state
as a harsh one, and a recognition of a more facile and honor-laden
condition as unnatural and unhealthy, but which flourishes because
of a kind of corruption, or at least of an excess which is in direct
contrast to the almost classic measure characteristic of Char's
moral attitude. The surrounding landscape is imbued not so much
with sentiment as with a deliberate ethical slant and moral purpose.
As an example, the essay "La Provence Point Oméga," and the
poem "Ruine d'Albion," although written specifically against the
atomic installations on the highland of Albion, loses none of its
moral pertinence from the fact that the protest was after all in vain;
the same is true of Char's recent declarations in keeping with what
we would now call ecological matters. Whatever the result of
Char's public statements has been, resentment is rarely present in
his writing: "Search as I may ... I find myself without ambition."
The refusal of an easy "well-being," the nonacceptance of honors,
the chosen isolation of a modest and out-of-the-way abode all fit in
with the countryside and its unforgiving light.

Even the names of the Vaucluse countryside enter the poems,
giving it a geographical continuity and, on a deeper level, an
interior situation. The little hill town of Le Thor, the slopes of
Aulan, the high bare ruins of Les Baux, Maussane, but also the
Névons, and the springtime flower of the Fontaine de Vaucluse,
famous for Petrarch's — all this is there, and yet the poetry looks
beyond, to a broader landscape, and within. The poet looks toward
the hill of La Petite-Pierre in Alsace, looks toward the Vosges and
the Pyrénées, as well as to the localities of concern, toward the
Greece of the Resistance, the Spain of the Civil War ("L'Hymne à
voix basse," "Par la bouche de l'engoulevent"), but also toward
the caves of Lascaux with their prehistoric drawings.

In the poems of *Le Nu perdu,* the landscape is almost entirely
that of the Vaucluse, of its vertical villages, perched on a hill like

Venasque ("A church frozen standing") in "Le Village vertical" (NP, 36), its ochre cliffs and dryness, its river Sorgue and the little stream of La Folie, its lost high town of Aerea, its mountain chain of the Luberon and the peaks whose delicate and jagged profile resembles lace: "Les Dentelles du Montmirail," leading to the bare windy height of the Mont Ventoux, whose name itself already contains the wind. The powerful poems of *Retour amont* (*Return Upland*), the first collection in *Le Nu perdu,* are arranged more or less from west to east, so says the poet, in the path of a return to a windy mountain which is, nevertheless, always interior, like the "summit of the heart" (FM, 45).

Yet, in spite of the abundance of proper names, the two volumes of 1972, *Le Nu perdu* and *La Nuit talismanique,* convey an indelible impression of a place beyond, or at least on the inside of that landscape. Of course all great poems move past their most evident landmarks, their figures, and their initial events, but these raise a particularly interesting problem by their very actuality and their concreteness, already hinted at in the first chapter of our study. Just as the picture of Francis and Louis Curel de la Sorgue with René Char, published in an anthology,[5] gives definition to the figure in the poem "Louis Curel de la Sorgue," just as the picture of René Char with his sisters and with Marthe, his childhood friend, published in that same volume, gives us a definite feeling about the poem "Marthe," or as, for those who have seen the picture of Louis Uni or Apollon in *Le Tombeau des secrets,* the character of Apollon in *Le Soleil des eaux* takes on new life, or even as a picture of those wanderers called Les Transparents itself gives a new scope to our reading of the poems in *Les Matinaux* called "Les Transparents," so each impression, verbal and visual, is multiplied and complicated. In our rereading, each of us, hearing the particular resonance not only of the poem but of the other tones we can remember, perceives also what we might have seen of a certain mountain or a river, drawing on all other mountains and all other rivers for the geographical setting, as we do on all other poems in our reading of one poem. If that superimpression is already sensible in our early reading of Char, it will be so much the more so in the later volumes, where the geography, while seeming more simply exposed to our view, takes on a progressively greater depth from its inner context.

CHAPTER 4

The Elements of the Poem

THE following very modest enterprise could be considered as taking the opposite direction from Gaston Bachelard's cosmic one in his discussion of the phenomenology of the elements and their importance for the literary imagination.[1] His examples of images taken from a wide range of poets illustrate not only facets of their attitude toward nature but also of his own. Even in his earlier works on the psychoanalysis of fire, on water and dream, on air and imagining and the two volumes on earth, as a representation of rest and as a representation of will, he did not choose the attitude of scientific objectivity evident in his other works; they were, rather, an interpretation of a literature of subjectivity, as is this one. My purpose here, however, is not to talk of the elements nor of literary imagination as such, but only of the forms in which the four elements are found and combined in Char's poetry, in all their profusion. In fact, for the reader who had no other approach to the poetry, this key might suffice for an initial inquiry.

For instance, we know that the alchemical tradition is largely based on the interplay of the elements: so we would expect that in the prose poems of *Abondance viendra* — several of which deal in part with alchemical themes — such play would be visible and frequent. And we might even expect that in a poet whose work is so intimately connected with nature, the images of air and water and earth and fire would take precedence over any other, in quantity and in importance. But the actuality seems to surpass by far any reasonable expectation: rather than making a series of lists (so many images of x and so many of y in ... whereas in ...) we have preferred to give a very general profile of the relevant images in each volume, in approximate order of publication, stressing a few individual poems throughout.

Quand les conséquences ne sont plus niées, le poème respire, dit qu'il a
obtenu son aire. Iris rescapé de la crue des eaux.

When the consequences are no longer denied, the poem breathes, says it
has reached its domain. An iris saved from the swell of waters. (SP, 33)

At the outset, we should remember that traditionally the study of
elements is also a study of contrasts: one might with some profit
analyze the sorts of contrasts in the entire work of Char, but that
general analysis would seem far too detailed and yet too dispersed
to have any effect upon our reading. And if we were to discuss
nature images in René Char,[2] we would lose the structural interest
of contrasts altogether. This study is meant to demonstrate a possible convergence of the concrete and the systematic, the natural and
the intellectual, the conscious and the unconscious. For it is clear
that, no matter how late Bachelard became acquainted with the
work of Jung,[3] still, the collective unconscious with its impulses
and its storehouse of universal similarity as represented in mythol-
ogy and literature is implied in such a study. In this case the reading
will start from the surface of the text where we glimpse this theme,
making no pretense of a complete taxonomy.

A further reason for choosing the elements as an alternative
entrance to the poetry is their substantiality; since they are not
scientific categories, they carry with them all the weight of tradition. Nor are they reductive, but rather they hint at something
beyond themselves. Of course, to a great extent, all Char's greatest
texts move from a concrete or material realm or an actual representation to an interior or metaphysical meditation, as was exemplified in the preceding chapter on interior and exterior architecture. The essential importance of the role played by the four elements is closely related to that progress, for if each of the elements
has its own reverberation — within the range of references exactly
analyzed at such length by Bachelard — it has also its own particular accumulation of meaning inside the texts of one poet. Char's
use of water is, for example, of a great range and a still greater
depth: our illustrations here cannot hope to do justice to that
range, or to that depth, which they only suggest.

Finally, it must be said that in the case of René Char, the order of
things is hallucinatory or unexpected, and so each element changes
slightly, depending on its insertion in the texts which include it, as

do the texts in the varied collections in which they are included. Perspectives vary, light shifts, and the vision of the reader must be as adaptable as that of the poet, whose subtlety he must appreciate and approximate as best he can. Certain lines may occur and recur in differing contexts, and, as Char says, thought is never simple. So for example, *Dans la pluie giboyeuse,* apparently situated under the sign of water — judging from the title — is in fact just as concerned with the other elements, including fire, whereas *Retour amont* — in which the ambiguity of earth and water is already included in the title — concerns water as much as the mountain.

I   Le Marteau sans maître (The Hammer With No Master)

General images of water with no specific personal associations seem to hold an overall importance in this early volume, whereas in later ones the water images are above all associated with a series of various female figures. We might compare the abundance of liquid imagery itself in this first major volume to the alchemist's *materia prima,* the original and undifferentiated matter on which subsequent experiments are made, and from which the most valuable result is to be coaxed, the primal liquid source of all things or the *magna mater.* In the first version of *Arsenal,*[4] in an unpublished poem called "L'Embaumé" ("The Embalmed"), a dead sea appears, explicitly dominant — in the rhythm of its heartbeat, only implied — even over the hardest matter, as we see, "La mer morte sans condition/BATTRE par coeur toutes les pierres" ("The unconditionally dead sea/TO BEAT by heart all the stones"). The particularly heavy water here suggests — although perhaps only to this reader — a woman asleep, a dead mother, as in the frequent play on words of "mère" and "mer," familiar to French readers since medieval times. The same suggestion is made in regard to those sleeping waters in "Eaux-mères," one of the texts in *Abondance viendra,* and a prose poem heavy with alchemical images (MM, 101). The first poem in the series, called "L'Eclaircie" ("Clearing") — an evocative title to open a series of poems — begins with an invocation to the *sources* or the springs, which are here placed in direct parallel with "Wandering Signs of Intelligence," the two terms, of spring and intelligence or understanding, rich in their interrelations, a possible erotic suggestion of future birth: "Fury has ravaged your nubile stomach . . ." and the suggestion of a stable "sea." The contrary themes of birth and death, each as a "voyage by water," are mingled here, as they often are by tradition.

More interesting is the association of the ocean with vision in a brief poem, "A L'Horizon," of *Le Tombeau des secrets*,[5] whose two major elements form also the focus of the short early poem "Bel édifice et les pressentiments." We might compare the two texts:

"A L'Horizon"

Ceux qui partent pour les nuages
Croient solide comme un roc
A l'avenir de la mer
Ouverte à l'oeil unique.

"On the Horizon"

Those who depart for the clouds
Believe with the firmness of a rock
In the future of the sea
Open to the lone eye.

"Bel édifice et les pressentiments"

J'écoute marcher dans mes jambes
La mer morte vagues par-dessus tête

. . . .

Des yeux purs dans les bois
Cherchent en pleurant la tête habitable.

"Fine Building and Forebodings"

I hear moving in my steps a sea long-dead
Waves overhead

. . . .

Pure eyes in the woods
Seek weeping the head to dwell in.   (MM, 28)

But in general, even here, as will be the case in Char's later works, the themes of departure and freedom are suggested by the elements of air, particularly in the form of breath. One of the poems (dated 1930) in *Le Tombeau des secrets* on the theme of freedom — "Chaque instant de ma tête/délivré de la terre/La force de chanter à tue-tête" ("Each instant of my head/freed from the earth/The strength to sing full blast") — bears a footnote saying the poem is not "commemorative" but rather "contradictory," not witty but rather "respiratory." Now the recurrence of such phrases as the "predilection of oxygen" (MM, 26), the description of "breathing like a plant" (MM, 22), a sort of spherical breathing said to enter into peace (MM, 8), the "aspirant vulnérable" (MM, 21), and the "relais de la respiration" (MM, 27), are not only typical but significant. Space must be left or then created around the poet, and the element of air is for that reason of an importance second only to water as the source. This theme is frequent in the German poet Hölderlin: "I must have space about me ... ," says Empedocles from the play by that name, where the philosopher hero bids his disciple farewell as, later, Char describes Rimbaud bidding farewell to his own poetic disciples. Also in Char's work, the notion of leave-taking often meets the element of air and the notion of space. "Farewell forever to this sparkling space," we read, or "giving leave to the wind."

The elements are found increasingly in combination with each other; the complexity of representation is greater than before. In the two-line poem "Voici," from *Arsenal,* previously discussed as the successful condensation of a longer poem, all the images work in the same direction, toward an erotic reading. Thus the "foam" which permits an ambivalent deciphering: "écume/écumeur," combines with vapor and smoke ("vapeurs en détresse") to suggest sexual ardor, the steaming underclothes in correspondence with the star's hot rosy brilliance, and the white rose suggesting by reversal a white flame ("étoile rose et rose blanche"), and suggesting also white undergarments, pink, however, with the color of the heat or the flame. Even what a line of this poem calls "minor pools" can give off this smoke if heated to the right temperature, thus neatly combining the elements of water, air, and fire.

More involved combinations, often of all four elements, are found in the *Poèmes militants* as well as in *Abondance viendra,* precisely in an abundance worth mentioning. In the initial poem of the former volume, fittingly entitled "La Luxure" ("Lust"), a profusion of torrents and sweats announces a central fire after a fluvial necropolis and a deluge of water diviners, while a dreamer (a true "fanatic of clouds") is able to throw the landscape into disorder without any actual "sliding of the terrain" of his conscious-

ness. Here the intense solidity of the earth ("terre/terrain"), conveying the same idea as that of keeping two feet on the ground,
contrasts sharply with the imagination of the air, as in Bachelard's
title *L'Air et les songes* (*Air and Dreams*): the liquid predecessors of
the central fire contrast with it topologically (surface to center) and
substantially by the medium of the elements (water to hearth). The
next poem, whose title "Métaux refroidis" ("Cooled Metals")
reiterates the alchemical theme only adumbrated before, using the
images of lightning and of "nocturnal gold" — that is, the gold not
to be seen or created in daylight. Again a call to freedom through
the air is heard: "Habitant des espaces mobiles de l'amour . . .
Libérateur du cercle" ("Dweller of the mobile spaces of love . . .
Liberator of the circle"), while a far-off and nebulous head is
threatened by water and fire: swamps conspire to sink it, dynamite
to pulverize it. Poetic value is clearly placed on the night gold
sunken in the earth like fire, and on the flowering of space, these
two images joined by one of the oldest legendary associations of
all, the alchemical and the mythological.

Even the title concerning the hammer takes on a fuller meaning
in relation to alchemical imagery, as we learn from Mircea Eliade's
discussion of the forge and alchemy, of the natural work as it is
allied with the work of the earth.[6] In Char's thought, the hammer is
associated also with Wotan ("Odin le Roc"), and his legendary
strength with the natural work — thus the hammer is related to the
sickle, the scythe, and the rhythm of work in the field, under the
sun, relieved by the nourishment of water: so the work on the earth
and that under the air, mingled with breath, are joined to water and
to fire. Always the crimson and fiery furnace of the birth of new
gold — seen at the end of one poem: "sources rouges" — is implicitly compared to the work of poetry. The gold, or the poem, is
hidden that it may bring forth fruit, like an operation in which all
the more value is conferred in proportion to the secrecy of the
operation. Real gold was always, according to Paracelsus and
others, to be differentiated from the common gold ("aureum
vulgi") by its lack of exposure. The poem ends with an invocation
to one tree in its eternal growing, so that natural expansion is implicitly likened here to the alchemical. Within the same volume, in
such poems as "Chaîne" and "Confronts" — whose titles already
indicate a connection between factors — references to the four elements are closely intertwined. In particular, "Confronts," intricate

and dense, is a masterpiece of quadruple confrontation, opening as
it does with two lines again signaling that central fire where the perfect alchemical gold is created:

>Dans le juste milieu de la roche et du sable
>de l'eau et du feu des cris et du silence
>universels
>Parfait comme l'or
>
>. . . . .
>
>Dehors
>La terre s'ouvre
>L'homme est tué
>L'air se referme
>
>. . . . .
>
>Les fainéants crépitent avec les flammes du bûcher . . .

>In the golden mean of universal rock and sand
>of water and fire of cries and of silence
>Perfect as gold
>
>. . . . .
>
>Outside
>The earth opens
>Man is killed
>Air closes back up
>
>. . . . .
>
>The idlers crackle with the flames . . .

It is as if the earth were breathing, in the middle of the elements
represented by rock and sand, water, and earth. In this scene, quiet
and crepuscular, man will perhaps incarnate light, in a trans-
mutation by fire after the union of the elements under their temporary disguises, for he is said to pass above "colors" and crystals,
the many masks of the universal essence of things. Later, Char will
not have quite this view of the universe, and the obvious references
to alchemy will be fewer, but his pleasure in confronting one element with another will remain unaltered. These "confrontations"
used as a title ("Confronts") are mirrored later in his titles, for instance, in the heading "substantial allies," that is, the persons and
painters whose work accompanies his own, and in that of the
"mortal partner," as each artist is the partner of the next. As all the

themes are themselves allied, either visibly or by implication, these two are joined in the overarching theme of the meeting between persons and elements, contradictory and complementary. The play *Claire* will show the enduring hope of encounter, represented in the natural relation between river and air, clarity and earth, an encounter finding its parallel in the human realm in the intensity of "Le Visage nuptial," or the nuptial countenance which, once glimpsed, remains throughout Char's work and thought. This early poem and the others like it later demonstrate the joining of elements, culminating in the incarnation of light itself, then reflected in the meeting of two human presences.

In *Abondance viendra,* there are the juxtapositions to be expected in a group of poems based, whether remotely or directly, on alchemical themes, such as those of earth and air, water and sun, air and fire: for example, "l'espèce fulgurante de grain solaire" ("the fulgurant species of sun squall") ((MM, 100) or "Le souffle abdiquera sur la cendre" ("Breath will abdicate on ashes") (MM, 112), the latter coming from a poem whose title is again indicative of the fitting of one element into another: after the "confrontation," an integration. The poem "Intégration" is centered explicitly this time on an enclosed ocean, like the first aspect of water discussed here, a *magna mater* as the source for the poem:

Banquises indissolubles, dans vos mers cloturées se résorbe la honte. Songes tirés des perversions immortelles, juste cible au bas du ventre qui déferle. . . .

Indissoluble ice floes, in your enclosed seas shame is reabsorbed. Dreams drawn from immortal perversions, narrow target at the base of the stomach that unfurls. . . . (MM, 112)

Let us take one final example: in the poem "Domaine," the four elements are contained, as boiling letters (thus, water and fire) are written in the air, a rainbow is contrasted with sand (air, earth), and a match afire leads to the idea of lava (water, and fire), thus explaining the ambivalent line: "C'est la lave finale" ("It's the final lava") (MM, 111), with which the idea of washing ("laver") is inextricably bound. In this domain, or at this source — for this seems to be, linguistically and substantially, the most intricate of the poems in this volume and, with "Crésus," the poem on gold, the richest — air is played against sand, fire against water, and boiling letters against boiling lava, both a combination of fire and liquid. The poem begins with an appeal to fecundation ("Tombe mars fécond") and it is as if the text itself were an answer to that appeal, fecund in contrasts and elements, the source for a later poetry of these same elements.

II Fureur et mystère (Furor and Mystery)

Much of this volume is made up of Char's wartime journal (*Feuillets d'Hypnos*), and so the fury is an active one, based on experience, carrying over to some extent into the writing of poetry which is also related to the other half of the title, made up as the poem is of rage and of mystery. In many of these texts, the element of water occurs alone, no longer, however, as a representation of the *magna mater* but rather as a fountain, a well, a river, or a stream, and each text has a form appropriate to its substance. The poem of the fountain, like the Fontaine de Vaucluse in its swell, rushes forward in what Char calls "Les Premiers instants," the first moments of freshness, like an endless triumph over everything dry and dull:

Les Premiers instants

Nous regardions couler devant nous l'eau grandissante. Elle effaçait d'un coup la montagne, se chassant de ses flancs maternels. Ce n'était pas un torrent qui s'offrait à son destin mais une bête ineffable dont nous devenions la parole et la substance. Elle nous tenait amoureux sur l'arc tout-puissant de son imagination. Quelle intervention eût pu nous contraindre? La modicité quotidienne avait fui, le sang jeté était rendu à sa chaleur. Adoptés par l'ouvert, poncés jusqu'à l'invisible, nous étions une victoire qui ne prendrait jamais fin.

The First Moments

We were watching the water as it flowed, increasing before us. It effaced the mountain suddenly, expelling itself from her maternal side. Not a torrent submitting to its fate but an ineffable beast whose word and substance we became. It held us amorous on the all-powerful arch of its imagination. What intervention could have constrained us? Daily tameness had fled, blood cast aside was rendered to its heat. Adopted by the open, abraded to invisibility, we were a victory which would never end. (FM, 213)

We quote that poem in its entirety, as having a profusion all its own, interesting for its difference from a poem of the well, for example, which shows depth rather than abundance, intensity rather than outpouring; these waters resound instead of flowing, their resonance is autumnal instead of springlike: "Eaux de verte foudre qui sonnent l'extase du visage aimé, eaux cousues de vieux crimes, eaux amorphes, eaux saccagées d'un proche sacre..." ("Waters of green lightning ringing the ecstasy of the loved face, waters sewn with old crimes, amorphous, waters plundered by a near consecration...") (FM, 30).

Both poems in their turn differ from the poem of the Sorgue, called "A Song for Yvonne,"[7] where rhyme and repetition create an easy current, swift flowing and sure, whose force culminates in a prayer for energy and for freedom: "Rivière au coeur jamais détruit dans ce monde fou de prison,/Garde-nous violent et ami des abeilles de l'horizon" ("River with heart never destroyed in this world crazy for prison,/Keep us violent and a friend to the bees of the horizon") ([JG] FM, 211). And finally, "Fastes," the greatest of these poems of water which has not the feel of the Vaucluse, is the poem of a sea in its flux, like the ebb and flow of a season and of a love. The three paragraphs describe the three stages of the sentiment which they record like the *Fasti* of Ovid to which the title refers, these tablets inscribed with a memorable event. First the couple who are themselves like an ocean: "nous qui étions silence, sympathie, liberté triste, mer plus encore que la mer" ("we who were silence, sympathy, sorrowful freedom, were sea still more than the sea") (FM, 209). The "we" then splits in two, while the verbs remain detemporized by the water imagery: "L'été chantait et ton coeur nageait loin de lui" ("Summer was singing and your heart swam far from it"). The form of the three paragraphs is mirrored in the triple beginning of the final paragraph, where also the sea has receded to such an extent that even the verbs have lost the liquid connotations: "Les ans passèrent. Les orages moururent. Le monde s'en alla" ("The years passed. The storms died down. The world went its way"). The last sentence of the poem takes up for the third time the triplet structure in its tragic paradox: "Je t'aimais, changeant en tout, fidèle à toi" ("I loved you, changing in everything, faithful to you"). Now the formal contrast with the verbal expression of a river or a fountain or a well is clear. For the poem of the river Sorgue just quoted flows through a current of rhymed couplets,whereas the poem of the Fontaine de Vaucluse spills out in one tumultuous paragraph as if it were itself made up of "the first moments," like a great waterfall, whereas the poem of the well is represented on the page by an invocation to the waters and a second, deeper paragraph of meditation. Each of these forms, visible but unobtrusive, is brought to the attention only by its implicit juxtaposition with the others in the whole series of water poems. We see now the perfect tripartite structure of "Fastes," as it recedes from the surface in three stages, from an external and seasonal desertion toward the poet's interior fidelity in spite of the changing seasons, a fidelity not only personal in its nature but poetic. He is above all faithful to the poem.[8] There is, it seems to us, no better example of the formal and psychological range of texts devoted to a single element in all of Char's work than this group of four poems.

The double and triple combinations of elements in this period create certain patterns revelatory of an attitude and a poetic character. With the lightness befitting a poem explicitly described as spellbound — "Envoûtement à la Renardière" ("Bewitchment at the Renardière") — the profile of a woman loved is sketched by the simplest contact of air and sun:

... votre visage, — tel est-il, qu'il soit toujours, — si libre qu'à son contact le cerne infini de l'air se plissait, s'entr'ouvrant à ma rencontre, me vêtait des beaux quartiers de votre imagination. Je demeurais là, entièrement inconnu de moi-même, dans votre moulin à soleil....

...your face, — as it is, may it always be, — so free that at its touch air's infinite ring crumpled, half-opening as I met it, clothing me with the fine streets of your imagination. I remained there, entirely unknown to myself, in your sun mill.... (FM, 24)

Many texts partake of the lightness of air: on a hill, a bright morning, with "filaments of wings" and the "temptation to cry aloud" ("Chérir Thouzon"); closely allied to the poem just quoted, the poem called "Jeunesse" ("Youth") brings a breeze and a freshness sufficient to overcome the weight of the past. Here, by implication, time has, like a fire, consumed the past metaphorically, until nothing remains but ashes blown away by wind and water in a merciful erosion:

Loin de l'embuscade des tuiles et de l'aumône des calvaires, vous vous donnez naissance, otages des oiseaux, fontaines. La pente de l'homme faite de la nausée de ses cendres, de l'homme en lutte avec sa providence vindicative, ne suffit pas à vous désenchanter.... Le chant finit l'exil. La brise des agneaux ramène la vie neuve.

Far from the tiles' ambush and the calvaries' alms, you give yourselves of birth, hostages of the birds, fountains. The slope of man, made from his ashes' nausea, of man struggling against his vindictive providence, is not enough to disenchant you.... Song terminates exile. The lambs' breeze brings back new life. (FM, 25)

This text should be compared with "Front de la rose," where again, the trace left by fire (ashes) and the presence of wind and water construct the poem's movement. Exile is overcome within the poem, thanks to the wind, in a pagan reconsecration of the universe by the elements of nature.

Quite another mood is responsible for the intensity of contrast between fire and water in the poem "Fréquence," a duet of the natural and the human at work, and at leisure, where the feeling of the poem points to more than is said, as if a space had been left, perhaps for rage as well as for mystery:

"Fréquence"

Tout le jour, assistant l'homme, le fer a appliqué son torse sur la boue enflammée de la forge. A la longue, leurs jarrets jumeaux ont fait éclater la mince nuit du métal à l'étroit sous la terre.

L'homme sans se hâter quitte le travail. Il plonge une dernière fois ses bras dans le flanc assombri de la rivière. Saura-t-il enfin saisir le bourdon glacé des algues?

"Frequency"

All day, helping man, the iron applied its body to the flaming mud of the forge. Finally, their twin muscles caused the thin night of metal confined in the earth to burst forth.

With no haste, the man leaves his work. He plunges his arm one last time into the darkened side of the river. Will he finally be able to grasp the icy hum of algae? (FM, 23)

The resonance of the final question, unanswered as it must remain, is prolonged by the previous subterranean reference: the algae reside in the water like the metal underground. The two paragraphs are set opposite to each other, as the triumphant images of heat and radiance ("enflammé ... éclaté"), once buried under the earth, now come to light, placed in sharp relief against the strong images of cold ("rivière ... glacé") and of darkness (even the sounds are somber: "flanc assombri"). In the same fashion, the successful work in the first description ("ont fait éclater") is placed against the leisure and the interrogation of the second ("Saura-t-il enfin saisir . . ."), its sibilants, the adverbs in each part signaling the time the process has taken or will take: "A la longue ... enfin." The algae may or may not eventually be seized, whereas the metal has, in actuality, already burst forth from the earth, as elegant in its thin lines as the poet's chosen iron, or "fer," and bearing still the protection of the underground hideout to which the somber side of the river corresponds. Even a physical correspondence is suggested between the man, the iron, and the river: the "torse" and the calves of the former two correspond to the "flanc" of the river. Time is made for the realization of all these correspondences by the man's lack of haste in leaving his work: the poem moves slowly, with the result that the elements are given their proper room and their distinctness from each other. The work of unearthing the precious metal of a poem cannot be hurried, as the poet points out repeatedly — the fire and the flow of poetry form the true concern of this "devoir."

Discussion of this volume should culminate with the epic love poem of 1938, "Le Visage nuptial" ("The Nuptial Countenance"), because of its length and its importance: all the elements converge within its majestic space. The entire poem can be read as a triumph of the traditional redemptive element of water over a "dead sand" and a "desert body," by means of the very strength of the love itself. Here our path follows in particular detail only the elements of water and air or breath in their opposition to the dryness, separation, and sterility connected by the images of sand and desert.

In order to illustrate Char's mastery of sound in the stressing of sense, any number of poems could be chosen; one might discuss how the hot morning air of a text filled with bees itself vibrates like a buzzing on the page, or how the perception of a landscape from a summit determines the configuration of certain audible elements, how the metallic images of *Le Marteau sans maître* strike as harsh sounds in its poems, or how, on the contrary, the gentlest love poems such as "La Chambre dans l'espace" ("The Room in Space") merge images of feathers and delicate crafting with whispered voices, befitting the lightness of the air. Instead let me offer as a model a brief discussion of perhaps the greatest of Char's poems, a poem I have discussed at length elsewhere — "Cycle of the Warring Couple," in *The Presence of René Char* (Princeton, 1976) — but which deserves its own volume apart. "Le Visage nuptial" carries within itself its own landscape, from a flowing spring to a stubble of wheat, from a desert to a mountain height.

The text contrasts liquid and dry sonorities, with the former revealing itself the stronger. The line of conquest leads from the most quiet of intimacies to the final resounding and double triumph of love over the sterile and loveless landscape.

The poem opens with a couple's dismissal to the group escorting them, the "indices" of a past experience and therefore to be rejected, so that the present may be undetermined and spacious before the two in their "nuptial countenance." The negation of the past in favor of the present setting is harsh, again marked in sibilants and stops: "A *p*résent *d*isparais, mon e*s*corte, *deb*out *d*ans la *d*i*s*tance;/La *d*ou*c*eur *d*u nom*b*re vient *d*e *s*e *d*é*t*ruire./ ... /*T*out vous en*t*raîne, *t*ri*s*te*s*se ob*s*é*q*uieuse" ("Now let my escort disappear, standing far off into the distance;/ Numbers have lost their sweetness./ ... /Everything summons you away, fawning sorrow") (FM, 58). The contrast of these lines with the long and muted resonance of the soft fricative and nasal sounds of the brief following line is striking: "J'aime" ("I am in love"). Now, as if the resonance of that sound had summoned it, the water which will finally triumph over everything else in the poem is heard both at its source and in all its weight: here the syllables are heavy and slow moving, in a violent change of sound from the beginning sibilant stops in their rapid succession to this dark fullness: "L'*eau* est lour*d*e à un *j*our de la *s*our*c*e" ("Water is heavy at a day's flow from the spring"). All moves with a slow sensuality here: the "slow branches" waving over the spring have even in their sound: "*len*tes br*an*ches," the obscurity given by the nasal quality appropriate to the shade from which the illumination of the love will rise. This integral heaviness is opposed throughout the poem not only to the intensity of the love but to the dry precision of the flint and the separateness of the grains of sand over which the final triumph takes place: in the flint and its setting we hear once more the stressed sibilants of the beginning (marked with small caps): "Le silex frissonnait sous les sarments de l'espace" (The flint was trembling under the vine-shoots of space") (FM, 60). With the sterility of the sand are allied a certain celestial aridity and effort: "le sable mort," "le ciel aride," "le pain suffoque" as well as the moral and spiritual desiccation refused by the love, which is always associated with the flowing of a source: "l'afflux de rosée" clearly interpretable on the erotic level, but transmuted also to the metaphoric level of renewal. After the aridity and the suffocation just illustrated, a catalog of sterile images hisses its way down the page in fricatives (marked with italics) and sibilants, denied in every case by the prefix: "I shall not see":

> Je ne verrai pas tes *f*lancs, ces essaims de
> *f*aim, se dessécher, s'emplir de ronces;
> Je ne verrai pas l'empuse te succéder dans ta serre;
> . . . .
> Je ne verrai pas la race de notre liberté
> servilement se suffire.

> I shall not see your sides, those swarms of
> hunger, dry up, be overrun with brambles;
> I shall not see the mantis replace you in your greenhouse;
> . . . .
> I shall not see our freedom's lineage servile
> in self-sufficiency.

Against this desert and this desertion — "le corps désert" ("the desert body"); "guérir de la désertion" ("cure from desertion") — the flow of the stream and of the storms suffices: "Ruisseaux . . . Mêlez votre acheminement aux orages de qui sut guérir de la désertion" ("Streams . . . Mingle your going with his tempests, who could heal desertion"). And in the next-to-last stanza, the poem itself seems to rise with the poet from the sterile depths toward an even height, far above the unimaginative level of the world left behind: "nous sommes montés au plateau" ("we have climbed upland"). Here the water, "l'*eau*," in its rounded syllable is included once more — "plat*eau*," and it is associated with a now always future bounty, that of the "afflux de rosée" ("the abounding dew") which finally saves the poem. To the water's depth the mountain's height replies, as the all-important notion of "up-stream" is absorbed into the "upland" of the expression "amont." This poem can be seen as prefacing the collection *Retour amont*, with its "retour compact" being the necessary prelude to that other return, as the genuine is opposed to the pretended in the body of the poem: "Assez maudit le havre des simulacres nupti*au*x:/Je t*ou*che le f*on*d d'un ret*ou*r compact" ("Long enough condemned, the haven of nuptial semblances:/I touch the depths of a compact return"). Even here the water penetrates, and the heavy sounds associated with it: (*ou,* or *eau* or *au*), the last of which reappears even in the final participle of redemption: "le corps s*au*vé."

In the last stanza, the sibilants reappear quietly, with the sharp sounds of triumph: (*i, é*), and now that the "countenance" is saved from sterility, the echoes within the poem are welcomed and pro-longed even in their opposition: "voici/voici, mort/corps, femme/homme": "Voic*i* le sable mort, voic*i* le corps Sauvé:/La Femme resp*i*re, l'Homme se tient debout" ("This is the sand dead, this the body saved:/Woman breathes, Man stands upright") (FM, 58–60). [Again, the sibilants are marked with small caps, and the sharp vowels with italics.]

"Woman breathes, Man stands upright." Now the aspect of the element of air as freedom could be summed up by the line from a "militant poem": "Bouche d'air imagination" ("Mouth of air imagination"). The title, "Poèmes militants," conveys the same sense of activity as the general title of the volume as it hammers independently. Among other meanings, this indicates the heart still beating, so that the respiratory rhythm, of an automatic uneven-ness, fits the pattern here. "Trois respirations" ("Three Breaths") is the title given to a brief essay in *Recherche de la base et du sommet,* and "une respiration" is the title Char originally sug-gested for the book of translations recently undertaken with him. Like the image of the "athletic chest of the universe," this title indi-cates all that we have suggested here: evenness, determination, space, liberty.

Compare, from the same volume of essays, the following state-ments on the conjunction of energy and control: "Il nous faut une haleine à casser des vitres. Et pourtant il nous faut une haleine que nous puissions retenir longtemps" ("We must have a breath strong enough to break windows, but which we can hold a long time") (RBS, 172).

The importance of the simple concept of respiration for the entire body of Char's work is great: it is related to the rhythm of living and writing. It can be traced from the early images in *Le Marteau sans maître* (such as the relation of the "athletic chest of the universe" to the lines "You are in a rush to write/As if you were of a slower pace than life/ . . . /Hasten," which appear in the poem "Commune présence") to the "Trois respirations" in the collection *Recherche de la base et du sommet*. Now the regular contrast of inhalation and exhalation and the insertion of that regularity into the most minute and exacting, or the most exalted and epic, experiences alike might be taken as indicative of the constantly keen awareness of extremes and the fertile tension between them. We would certainly not go so far as to promulgate the psycho-physiological theories of André Spire on the subject of poetry and breathing and the necessary relations between them,[9] or any exaggerated conceptions of the relation of the corporal to the mental, but we are drawing attention to the image of respiration because of its place in Char's consciousness and for its representation of the automatic regulation of extremes in the *corpus* taken in both senses, body and work. The force symbolized by the breath of the speaker, "mon souffle," a breath echoed in the "lips of the fog" closing in over the couple, might be thus imagined as part of the "belt of mist" worn by the narrator, which predicts the belt of seasons in the poem "Seuil." The breath returns at the conclusion, the woman then breathing easily as her partner stands upright. To both, an energy is restored which makes their encounter the ideal model for a juncture of form and emotion, that is, for poetry itself, whose double this poem is.

Corresponding to the final posture of the man standing, both partners are now capitalized to show us that the "moi" and the "toi" of the first stanzas have now assumed a more general importance, a generic destiny beyond that of the individual, as the mountain height reached is beyond the desert sands of the land overcome and also beyond the spring, transcending even the source of water. Yet the echo of the water, the triumph of the breath throughout the stanzas of the poem are essential. Poetry is made up also of the smallest elements, and great poems include even in their detail the signs of their intimate concern.

III   Les Matinaux (The Matinals)

The matinal poems were given their name from their early morning light, filled more with luminosity and hope than with the fury and mystery of those preceding them. They are said by the poet to be situated on the more temperate side of his imagination:

"Les Matinaux vivraient, même si le soir, si le matin, n'existaient plus."
"The Matinals would live even if evening, morning no longer existed".
("Faire du chemin avec..." ["To Walk a While With..."]) (1976).

A. La Sieste blanche (White Siesta)

The poems of "La Sieste blanche" are songs "serving as corridors between our breath at rest and our strongest fevers." (Thus, according to our present concern, between air and fire.) In the first edition of a commentary on this collection,[10] Char describes these poems as "banal songs" of a biting blue color, with, however, a tiny wound in this fabric, but he modifies the final version to make it a "clement coloring," again turning from the physical description to the metaphoric. This tranquillity, in any case, is conducive to repose, and thus the title, as of a siesta taken in an open field, with clouds drifting over. Or a nap in which one does not sleep, by analogy with "nuit blanche," a sleepless night. The poems themselves appear airy, and only at the end of the collection does any hint of tragedy appear, in "Les Nuits justes" ("Righteous Nights"): "La gueule du ciel est blanche./Ce qui miroite, là, c'est toi,/Ma chute, mon amour, mon saccage" ("The sky's muzzle is white./You are what sparkles there,/My falling, my love, my devastation") (LM, 53). Here the white of the sky belies the final word, tense with destruction; the mixture of clarity and sadness is reminiscent of the preceding poem, concerned with rains and the windows on which they fall and through which we see them: "J'ai mal et je suis léger" ("I suffer and am light"). The lightness of clouds parallels the lightness of the suffering, understated. These are in general simple poems, whose sound and sense may not seem to carry far, until a second reading, where the snow of the Pyrénées is of a particular cold after the desert sands (LM, 40), where the water of a well seems salty as the sea, whereas the water's trembling is implicitly compared to tears. Again the physical aspect is transferred to a psychological attitude.

B. Le Consentement tacite (Tacit Consent)

To say even a few words on "Consentement tacite" is perhaps indiscreet, since a tacit consent should presumably not be unfolded. And yet the subject is suggested in "Pleinement" ("Fully"), the final poem of the collection following it, "Joue et dors" ("Play and Sleep") and suggested with a discretion we might well imitate, akin to the same lightness of air:

> Ce que nous avions vu flotter
> Bord à bord avec la douleur
> Etait là comme dans un nid,
> Et ses deux yeux nous unissaient
> Dans un naissant consentement.
>
> . . . .
>
> What we had seen floating
> Edge to edge with pain
> Was there as in a nest,
> And its two eyes bound us together
> In a nascent consent.
>
> . . . . (LM, 72)

This consent seems to apply not only to death and suffering, but to what complements them. The poem is called "Pleinement" ("Fully") which must surely include both sides of the feeling we have analyzed only partially.

The poems of the collection "Consentement tacite" each appear as profound as the texts of "La Sieste blanche" or of "Au-dessus du vent" ("Above the Wind") appear light: the alternation between slopes or aspects of the work is an essential part of their profile. Four of the seven poems have their base in a single element, whether presented or only implied, "L'Amoureuse en secret" ("Loving in Secret"), a text whose mood we have already observed, where a meal shared in love and in a calm sensuality, ends with an unforgettable comparison, of a tone as quiet as the secrecy in the title and the simplicity of the table, and yet with the same long-lasting resonance. The food is compared to the reed of an oboe — thus the vibrancy of sound is always contained, only potential — and the bed awaits with an equally reserved potentiality: "Un lit, très loin, sait-elle, patiente et tremble dans l'exil des draps odorants, comme un lac de montagne qui ne sera jamais abandonné'' (''She knows a bed, far off, awaits and trembles in the exile of sweet-smelling sheets, like a mountain lake never to be abandoned'') (LM, 57). The simultaneous peace and high intensity of the quiet ripples of the lake make the perfect echo to the unheard notes of the instrument. The poem directly preceding this one, ''Grège'' (''Greige''), takes its departure in an atmosphere equally vibrant, in which the brilliant sky blue where a potential storm is brewing makes a fitting background for the metaphor of risk and change. The air is the perfect medium for the clash of festival and death:

La Fête, c'est le ciel d'un bleu belliqueux et à la même seconde le temps au précipité orageux. C'est un risque dont le regard nous suit et nous maintient....

The Revels, a sky of bellicose blue and in the same instant, a season of stormy precipitate. A risk whose gaze follows and maintains us....

(LM 59)

Through the transparency of the element, the menace of death is felt, however, as devoid of tragedy: the circularity of the poem, beginning and ending with this word of Festival, reminds us of the poem ''Invitation,'' where the clouds summon, as if in a dance, the loves and the lovers who have no choice but to respond to the call which is also a call of death.

''Recours au ruisseau'' (''Recourse to the Stream'') continues the metaphor of risk from ''Grège'' and the quiet vibrancy of the images in ''L'Amoureuse en secret'' into the stream with its quivering plants: ''Sur l'aire du courant, dans les joncs agités, j'ai retracé ta ville'' (''On the surface of the current, among the quivering rushes, I retraced your town'') (LM, 61). The masons with all their competency doubt the value of poetic construction, whose progress is in any case different, since rebuilding takes place at every moment, higher up along the stream, of whose gravel the poet claims to have no need. His construction is other than theirs, and its outline can be perfectly traced in the ripples of its current without undermining its stability. For finally the sky itself is reflected in the river, and the two elements make a combined strength beyond that of ordinary habitations: this dwelling will finally be the sole possible "head to dwell in" or the mental habitation poetry seeks to reveal or to construct.

The final poem to consider in this light is "Les Lichens," which recounts a walk of the poet in a mountainous country with its secret breath, where every trace and every memory are lost, but where the "fullness of the wind" restores all the potentialities of giving and the certainties of love, as a recompense for separation and loss: as we have seen in a few other poems, the element of air lends always a majesty and space to Char's poems, akin to the profundity of suffering and redemption lent them by the element of water. Here the earth bounteously displays all its qualities as the poet sets out on an unspecified quest:

Je marchais parmi les bosses d'une terre écurée, les haleines secrètes, les plantes sans mémoire. La montagne se levait, flacon empli d'ombre qu'étreignait par instant le geste de la soif.... Nous allions nous séparer. Tu demeurerais sur le plateau des arômes et je pénétrerais dans le jardin du vide. Là, sous la sauvegarde des rochers, dans la plénitude du vent, je demanderais à la nuit véritable de disposer de mon sommeil pour accroître ton bonheur. Et tous les fruits t'appartiendraient.

I walked among the hummocks of a land scoured, the secret breaths, the plants without memory. The mountain rose up, a shadow-filled flask embraced now and again by the gesture of thirst.... We were going to separate. You would remain on the high plain of scents and I would enter the garden of the void. There, in the safekeeping of rocks, in the wind's fullness, I would place my sleep at the disposition of the true night for it to deepen your happiness. And all the fruits would be yours by right. (LM, 64)

The thirst here is answered also by the lake, the stream, and the sea of other poems, as the fruits depend on the fullness of wind and the generosity expressed elsewhere, in a mixture of warmth and sky, or fire and air. All these dense accumulations of feeling enter also into the tacit but real consent given by the poet to the universe.

C. La Paroi et la prairie (The Rock-Wall and the Meadow)

The two sets of texts making up this collection fit side by side. Each consists of four brief poems and a summary poem: the first set, "Lascaux," relates to the cave walls, and the second, "Quatre fascinants," to any meadow in Provence, thus together they join the prehistoric to the contemporary. The animal figures in the enclosed or "cultural" space and those in the open or natural space answer and complement each other. As we might expect, the poems of Lascaux are of a fierce intensity, extremely brief and thus heightened in tone by being set in a small space, while those of the meadow are at once more exposed and more delicate. Taken as a whole, this group of poems holds widespread appeal through its consistency of figures and of tone. The poems of animals are the most frequently quoted of all his texts: their perfect construction, instantly visible, sets them apart from the poems whose figures are harder to grasp, whose appeal is often more intellectual than instinctive.

To a surprising extent, the entire range of elements is gathered up in these poems: in this sense the collection is the opposite of the preceding one, where the elements, singly, lent each its particular flavor to the text. Here, on the other hand, the background element is subordinate to the animal mass profiled against it. A poem on the black deer drawing in Lascaux begins with a picture of water and sky, closely joined, with the latter seen as youth and softness by contrast with the old caverns of the earth: "Les eaux parlaient à l'oreille du ciel./Cerfs, vous avez franchi l'espace millénaire,/Des ténèbres du roc aux caresses de l'air" ("The waters spoke on into the sky's ear./Stag, you and you and you have crossed millennia, the space/From rock darkness to the air's caresses") ([JG] LM, 102). The natural picture is of less interest than the figures in the foreground, rather like the contrast between the two levels of Greek vase painting, or like the continuous playing against the melody of a Bach concerto. The last animal (an "unnameable beast" whom the poet identifies with wisdom, "her eyes filled with tears") belches into the rustic air (LM, 103), or a young horse, like springtime, covers the reeds with the foam of its "vaporous mane" (LM, 104): these tears, this foam, and this air link with the water and air of the preceding poem, of especial interest as they enhance the outline of the foreground figure, whether it is a beast of great bulk or of young energy.

Exactly the opposite is true of the summing-up poem of the Lascaux cycle, "Transir," whose brevity does not diminish its epic reach. It is again a question of the profile of these various works as they fit together: from the miniature to the large scale, and from the matinal to the nocturnal, as from the cavern to the meadow, the very extremes are essential to the poetic appeal, the latter term used here to include the meaning of the "appelants" in Char's play *Le Soleil des eaux*. They attract our interest and hold it. The poem opens by an invocation to the source of the multiple in man, a potentiality for the manifold which will be realized only tomorrow. (DEMAIN LE MULTIPLE.) The "chilling" in the title, that of the body numbed with cold, is not to last, for the poem will end with a heat as infinite as this chill is penetrating. Char explains the title as the "action of cold (or of fright . . .) that works on the spirit, on the heart, rather than on the body alone (as opposed to freezing). 'Chilling,' 'benumbing,' yes, but they do not give exactly the idea of this transitive cold, which is, I think, fecund."[11] The range of possibility, from the word "multiple" to the final word "infinie," is indeed unlimited, the epoch stretching backward and forward, further than the imagination's own reach. To fill the vast expanse of these brief poems, all the four elements are joined:

> Cette part jamais fixée, en nous sommeillante,
> d'où jaillira DEMAIN LE MULTIPLE.
> L'âge du renne, c'est-à-dire, l'âge du souffle.
> O vitre, ô givre, nature conquise, dedans fleurie,
> dehors détruite!
> . . . .
>
> Au soleil d'hiver quelques fagots noués et ma flamme
> au mur.
> Terre où je m'endors, espace où je m'éveille,
> qui viendra quand vous ne serez plus là?
> (*que deviendrai-je* m'est d'une chaleur
> presque infinie).

> This never stilled part, slumbering in us, from
> which will spring TOMORROW THE MANIFOLD.
> The age of the reindeer, — that is, the age of
> breathing. O window pane, o hoarfrost, o conquered
> nature, in flower within, outside destroyed!
> . . . .
>
> In the winter sunshine a few bundles of fagots and
> my fire by the wall.
> Earth on which I go to sleep, space into which I
> wake, who will come when you are no longer there?
> (*what shall I become* has for me an almost infinite
> warmth).
>   ([JG] LM, 105)

The breathing of reindeer is joined to that of man, the frost or outer sign of winter complements the sun, the flame, and the metaphysical heat of the question as to the future, as the earth for repose balances the active, waking space: these are not simple details, but the stuff of the poem itself, preparing the final unanswered question in its ardor and its sustained relevance. For the poet whose being and whose poems "are always in the act of becoming, they are never complete."[12]

Now the four poems of the meadow with its actual figures make up the other half of the diptych. The poem of the bull, which initiates the second half, continues the procession of cave pictures, leading history to the present spectacle. Each of these four "fascinators" entraps by its brilliance, and each presents a single element. The bright violence of the bull ring extends its own light beyond that of the day, like a spreading fire. The "sun with two like points" includes the matador's piercing blade as well as the horns of the bull, in a double wounding, like that of love.[13] A trout is seen only by the "transparent storms" in which it plunges (LM, 107); a serpent is seen only by his apparent fleeing, through all the caverns of earth, through wood and house; a lark is seen at the extremes of sunset and of dawn, its breath always said to match its free path in the sky.

In the final texts of the collection, profound waters engulf the whole, like an increasing flood. The path taken in the text bears the material descriptions of earth: "campagne rase," "talus." A lark sings in the gray sky and bubbles break the surface evenness of the waters; but the images of earth and air are all eventually to be absorbed by the "beauty of the deepwater" which closes the entire series, from the caves to the open. This conclusion implies the anxious interrogation of the text "Transir" as its only possible answer, for, as we will read in *Aromates chasseurs* of 1975: "La réponse interrogative est la réponse de l'être" ("The questioning answer is the answer of being") (AC, 18).

D. Le Rempart de brindilles (The Rampart of Twigs)

As we have noticed before, a convergence of elements often marks the densest poems and those widest in scope. The three poems written in the same month (March, 1953) attain together one of the "initiating summits" from which the expanse of the poet's work can be seen.[14] The expression, clearly related to the idea of the

poet as a "great beginner" of things, and as a "seeing summit,"
may be applied to some of Char's greatest texts.

"L'Inoffensif" consists of a lament at the day's ending, in which
human tears and nature's torrential currents correspond, like fire-
works and the sun, like the sky's darkness and a man's blindness:
human feelings and human creations answer natural forces:

> Je pleure quand le soleil se couche parce qu'il te dérobe à ma vue et
> parce que je ne sais pas m'accorder avec ses rivaux nocturnes.
> . . . .
> Il fait nuit. Les artifices qui s'allument me trouvent aveugle.

> I weep when the sun sets, because he screens
> you from my sight and because I never can
> come to terms with his nocturnal rivals.
> . . . .
> It is night. The kindling lures find me blind.
>   ([JG] LM, 120)

Water, fire, air, and earth are joined here in a tableau combining
sentiment and spectacle toward the final question in its ambiguous
allusion to one or the other, or to both. Many of Char's poems con-
tain questions and statements of a tense ambivalence: elsewhere I
have called them texts of the threshold, as they are, both themati-
cally and formally, stretched between two poles: light and dark, the
human and the natural, joy and grief.

The poem "Front de la rose" ("Brow of the Rose") is an
extraordinary example of the way in which an actual setting realizes
its potentiality for a metaphysical statement. The elements are integrated into the poem's base, like age-old equivalents of the oppositions, composing its double texture: hard and soft, morning and
shadows. These dominate even over the metaphorical line leading
from the words "I weep" through the moments of despair ("I
never can come to terms" . . . "your head cut off" and of corresponding images, such as blindness) to the final word
"shadows." The construction of the text parallels that of the substance: a lament is heard in the present ("I weep . . . I cease . . . it is
night") instantly followed by what seems to be a denial of all past
anguished moments, except this one: "I wept only once, really."
The two different moments of the poem, anguish and a calm reflec-

tion on that anguish, are then followed by a question, asked in the perpetual present... "Which...?" resolved by a description of the morning and the shadows as the two moments of the same being, each constantly available. Yet this "solution" — if we are determined to have a solution — would not diminish the force of the initial lament, which weighs on the rest of the poem by its length and its eloquence. The "false rivals" of the original title,[15] were we to think of them as these two moments of opposite perception, matinal and nocturnal, are after all in a false opposition from the point of view of the threshold, over which we must be allowed to pass in both directions: from sun to tears and shadows or from the latter to the sun's reassurance, for water and fire are then each an essential part of the poem's orbit, like hardness and softness or the feminine and the masculine elements.

"Front de la rose" ("Brow of the Rose"), the final poem of this series, is founded in just such a way on the elements. The poem moves rapidly from impersonal metaphorical commentary, from the breath remaining in a room with the smell of a rose — whose perfume would, says the poet, fan away even death — to a conclusion more personal, if still unspecified as to subject. Here the breath and the wind are both linked to texts of departure. The second paragraph comments on that idea of movement, now transposed from the abstraction of air and the unspecified subject of love and desire and linked to earth as well as to water:

> Celui qui marche sur la terre des pluies n'a rien à redouter de l'épine, dans les lieux finis ou hostiles. Mais s'il s'arrête et se recueille, malheur à lui! Blessé au vif, il vole en cendres, archer repris par la beauté.

> He who walks on the earth of rains has nothing to fear from the thorn, in places finite or hostile. But should he stop to meditate, woe to him! Wounded to the quick, he flies to ashes, archer recaptured by beauty. (LM, 123)

The threat of immobility is a threat by fire, implicitly compared to beauty's blaze itself, like the traditional association between the sun, whose beauty or whose dagger consumes mortal observers. Again the elements are inseparable from the text and are to some extent implied within it: for instance, "our giddy foreheads" implies the departure of water or sweat, not as the rose or its rereading (la rose → l'arrose) implies its presence. The reader has himself the responsibility of supplying the hidden element, like the action described in all the poems of the well, from which the curative water is raised.

E. L'Amie qui ne restait pas (The Friend Who Did Not Stay)

Other cases of the elements in their intensely felt presence abound in this group of poems. "Fièvre de la Petite-pierre d'Alsace" describes a walk on a burning forest expanse as if it were a sea journey, threatened by explosion and destruction, as the boat confronts the waves head on, "face aux lames." The journey is marked as tripartite, and in the first part, behind the "savage" ceiling of night, the very existence of a sky is questioned; as the boat waits anchored in the second part, it appears, and the "ascension" of the traveler is predicted. The final part, a recall of the varied passages of energy ("bond," "marche"), presents a general invocation of the human journey, over the "daily" ocean — entangled with the casting-lines of the passengers in other boats — and through the "mortal fire." Thus the passage is feverish, yet epic.

Often there is a passing allusion to one or the other element in the poem, such as a flame of energy or of knowledge, to which the human consciousness is often irrelevant: "Flamme à l'excès de son destin, qui tantôt m'amoindrit et tantôt me complète, vous émergez à l'instant près de moi, dauphin, salamandre, et je ne vous suis rien" ("Flame in excess of its fate, which now diminishes me and now again completes me, you emerge in this moment near me, dolphin, salamander, and I am nothing to you") (LM, 126). Or the fire of the baker's furnace, always compared to the poet's own creation, for which he must be present "when the bread comes from the oven" (LM, 141), even at the price of cutting short his human contacts ("brusquer les adieux"). Air is, on the other hand, a perfect background element, a relaxed contrast to the intensity of fire, and to the invigorating and nourishing power of water and of the living waters which are the source of the poem itself: "La source, notre endroit!" (The spring, our dwelling-place!") (LM, 130). Earth, the *arrière-pays* or the backcountry, is also the place of the mind's safest traverse, while water implies risk, suffering, and discovery, which is sometimes tragic: "Qui a creusé le puits et hisse l'eau gisante/Risque son coeur dans l'écart de ses mains" ("Whoever has dug the well and raises recumbent water/Risks his

heart in the disjoining of his hands") (NP, 30). In "Marmonnement" ("Mumbling") the poet finds his double in the wolf,
marginal to society, whose being resembles his own:

> Pour ne pas me rendre et pour m'y retrouver, je t'offense, mais combien
> je suis épris de toi, loup, qu'on dit à tort funèbre, pétri des secrets de mon
> arrière-pays. C'est dans une masse d'amour légendaire que tu laisses la
> déchaussure vierge, pourchassée de ton ongle. Loup, je t'appelle, mais tu
> n'as pas de réalité nommable. De plus, tu es inintelligible. Non-
> comparant, compensateur, que sais-je? Derrière ta course sans crinière, je
> saigne, je pleure, je m'enserre de terreur, j'oublie, je ris sous les arbres.
> Traque impitoyable où l'on s'acharne, où tout est mis en action contre la
> double proie: toi invisible et moi vivace.
> Continue, va, nous durons ensemble; et ensemble, bien que séparés,
> nous bondissons par-dessus le frisson de la suprême déception pour briser
> la glace des eaux vives et se reconnaître là.

> Not to surrender and so to take my bearings, I offend you, but how in
> love with you I am, wolf, wrongly called funereal, moulded with the
> secrets of my back country. In a mass of legendary love you leave the vir-
> gin, chased trace of your claw. Wolf, I call you, but you have no nameable
> reality. Moreover, you are unintelligible. By default, compensating, what
> else could I say? Behind your maneless running, I am bleeding, weeping; I
> gird myself with terror, I forget, I am laughing under the trees. Pitiless and
> unending pursuit, where all is set in motion against the double prey: you
> invisible and I perennial.
> Go on, we endure together; and together, although separate, we bound
> over the tremor of supreme deception to shatter the ice of quick waters and
> recognize ourselves there. (LM, 131)

The convergence of the elements remains a profound one particularly in the greatest poetry, for instance, in the series of poems
beginning with "Victoire éclair" ("Lightning Victory"), in which
the earth is ploughed over by birds and sowed by snakes. Pluto in
the sky is addressed, and the explosion in the poet, like that in
L'Effroi la joie, is related to a natural occurrence, that of lightning.
But here it is a question of love, and the balance of the poem
stresses by its sharpness — in substance and in sound — the value
of this experience, a flame by contrast with a slow and dull steadi-
ness, represented here under the guise of snow, one of the modifica-
tions of water:

Plus de second soi-même, de visage changeant, plus de
saison pour la flamme et de saison pour l'ombre!

Avec la lente neige descendent les lépreux.

Soudain l'amour, l'égal de la terreur,
D'une main jamais vue arrête l'incendie, redresse
le soleil, reconstruit l'Amie.

Rien n'annonçait une existence si forte.

No more second self, or changing face, no more
a season for flame and a season for shadow!

With the slow snow descend the lepers.

Suddenly love, terror's equal,
With hand never seen checks the fire, restores
the sun, reconstructs the Beloved.

Nothing gave notice of a life so strong.

([JG] LM, 137)

The poem is a victory of the fire, as a bolt of lightning is quickly
triumphant over the less rapid, less intense, and colder elements.
Nothing prepared this strength, however, or this poem, of such an
open illumination.

In keeping with the alternation of perspective, the following
poem "La Chambre dans l'espace" ("The Room in Space")
inscribes itself under the rubric of air, victor over the heaviness of
earth and the slowness of water. The intensity of fire was demon-
strated in the preceding poem, where all the elements were present.
The love poem here announces itself as a song, fresh and vigorous
in correspondence with the coming rain:

Tel le chant du ramier quand l'averse est prochaine — l'air se poudre de
pluie, de soleil revenant—, je m'éveille lavé, je fonds en m'élevant; je ven-
dange le ciel novice. . . .

Like the wood-pigeon's song when the shower is near — the air is pow-
dered with rain, with haunting sunshine—, I awake washed, I melt in
rising; I vintage the newcomer sky. . . . (LM, 138)

The narrator compares himself to a bit of earth, rather than any more solemn image, and the succeeding descriptions are also as light in form as in substance, thus plainly inscribed under the rubric of air: "L'aile de ton soupir met un duvet aux feuilles" ("The wing of your sigh makes the leaves downy") ([JG] LM, 138). The space in which this room is included is of a vast lightness.

As the title "Lightning Victory" pointed already to fire, and "The Room in Space," to the element of air, so the next title of what we are here considering as a trilogy refers to water: "Rapport de marée" ("Tide Ratio"). Beginning with a question related to "earth and sky," the poem then moves to a specific object, one branch, but soaked in a tepid water, like a raft without future, a perfect image of death. Unlike the explosion of lightning in "Victoire éclair" or the intensity of fire in "Transir," the entire atmosphere is one of quiet, of lingering and languishing. Only a glance — whether of the reader or of an observer placed within the poem, we cannot tell — makes any motion within this torpor. The level of this tide, the marks it leaves on the earth over which it sweeps, might be presumed to communicate with the sentiment, but the poem itself leads only toward separation and questioning: "Mais, cette fois, nous ne ferons pas route ensemble./Bien-aimée, derrière ma porte?" ("But this time we shall not travel together./Beloved, behind my door?") (LM, 139). The end is, like the beginning, a question, and the level of the water remains as uncertain and as changeable as the human heart: reading the poem, we mentally juxtapose it with "Fastes," where the heart was constant in spite of the tidal flux. Char's work is, as we see at each step of the way, its own universe, never free of tides, of the ebb and flow of feeling and of form. Once engaged in it, the reader develops his own fidelity, holding "in spite of everything."

Pourquoi la journée vole" ("Why the Day Flies"), the final poem of *L'Amie qui ne restait pas,* resumes the others, including all the elements seen now in a different light, and speaks at last for the poet:

Le poète s'appuie, durant le temps de sa vie, à quelque arbre, ou mer, ou talus, ou nuage d'une certaine teinte, un moment, si la circonstance le veut....

The poet leans, during his lifetime, on tree, or sea, or slope, or cloud of a certain hue, one instant, if circumstances wish it so.... (LM, 141)

But these are not his real world, nor are they unique, for "his love, his grasp, his happiness" have equivalents in every place, even those to which he will never go: his unique country is another, one to the side ("à côté") of this one, "du ciel qui vient d'être englouti" ("from the sky just swallowed up"). Although three elements make up his touchstones or, literally, points of support ("points d'appui"), his singleness is noticeably associated with the element of air, as we have already seen, in discussing the space which must be made about the poet, the leave which he must take from others. Yet the poem does not stop there; rather it returns from that other country by way of a terse abstract statement toward a metaphor of utter simplicity, based on the element of fire, complementary to the air of that other country, now disappeared:

> Le poète vivifie puis court au dénouement.
> Au soir, malgré sur sa joue plusieurs fossettes d'apprenti, c'est un passant courtois qui brusque les adieux pour être là quand le pain sort du four.

> The poet gives life, then hastens to the outcome.
> In the evening, in spite of several apprentice dimples on his cheek, he is a courteous passerby cutting short the farewells to be there when the bread comes out of the oven. (LM, 141)

The modest oven of the baker is chosen as the suitable recipient and place of passage for the poetry — like the *athanor* of its alchemical creation, that "foyer" or crucible Char mentions elsewhere, exigent in its timing and common to all, a presence at once unremarkable and miraculous.

F. Au-Dessus du vent (Above The Wind)

The poems of this collection are intended to be lighter than the wind; they could all be inscribed under the heading of air, and respond, in that sense, to the original poems of *Les Matinaux* in their clarity. The first of the poems sets the tone for them all: "Les prairies me disent ruisseau/Et les ruisseaux prairie./Le vent reste au nuage" ("The meadows say stream to me/And the streams, meadow./The wind stays with cloudy weather") (LM, 173). All the poems seem open, like those of the meadow in *La Paroi et la prairie*. This is not to say that they are free of sadness: in "L'Issue" ("The Outcome"), all light is extinguished, the poet loses his way and his "true time," limiting himself "to a cloudy sky" (LM, 175). Yet these clouds are still part of the air, and over them, the sun — associated as often in Char's imagination, with the work of the harvest — triumphs at last. One "issue" or way out from the clouds is thus of work, but the idea enters with the lightness of the clouds themselves, and a befitting brevity. For the poems are those of a "grège chaleur," a heat the color of raw silk.

As one might expect, these delicate poems are based each on one single element or a combination of two, as in the images of sky and sun, for example (LM, 175) or simply the paths of earth chosen always over the more direct highway, "La Route par les sentiers" ("The Road by the Paths," LM, 179), or then of the river and the sun, as in the seemingly transparent "Déclarer son nom" ("Declaring One's Name," 180).

Time and the flow of water are felt as the watchful ten year old remembers them, in a song faintly resonant with pain. The final question has no obvious answer other than the correspondence of the child's excitement with the water wheel of the river Sorgue as it turns the waters in their rushing into a "white fire." Char is particularly sensitive to what he calls the child's *en-avant,* the mysterious future developing in the young. Here the personality (or the name) has not yet been declared, and its very potentiality, sensed in the question, is the source of poetry. (We are reminded of the question "What shall I become?" in the poem "Transir.")

The next poems also play one element against another, first earth against water and then air against earth; "Traverse" ("Short Cut") pictures a hill descending in a torrent like a gully wet with rain, or then a river turning toward the poet for his brief self-contemplation and its reflection: "La face rose de l'ornière tourne deux fois vers lui l'onde de son miroir. La méchanceté dort. Il est tel qu'il se rêvait" ("The pink face of the gully turns twice toward him the wave of its mirror. Wickedness sleeps. He is as he dreamed himself to be" (LM, 181). "Si..." ("If...") shows a grim moment of despair, and a loss of our own countryside, while "the sky rotted"; the bareness and the decay of this moment are placed in our uncertain future by the title itself, and this space created around the poet is seen in its darkest light. On the opposite side, each of these poems seems to have its brighter or its darker double. "Eros suspendu" ("Eros Suspended") has in its rhythm and images a Rimbaldian resonance, particularly reminiscent of his prose poem "Aube" ("la

déesse ... elle fuyait parmi les clochers et les dômes ... je l'ai
entourée avec ses voiles amassés, et j'ai senti un peu son immense
corps''):

> Je te vis, la première et la seule, divine femelle dans les sphères boule-
> versées. Je déchirai ta robe d'infini, te ramenai nue sur mon sol. L'humus
> mobile de la terre fut partout.
> Nous volons, disent tes servantes, dans l'espace cruel, — au chant de ma
> trompette rouge.

> I saw you, the first and the only one, divine female in the greatly dis-
> turbed spheres. I tore your dress of infinity, brought you back naked onto
> my soil. The mobile humus of the earth was everywhere.
> We are flying, say your servants, in cruel space, — to the song of my red
> trumpet. (LM, 186)

As the blaring of the crimson trumpet sounds like the cruelty of
space vivid against the night, so the triple grandeur of sky and
space and the infinite complement the specificity of the ground
with its soil, finally triumphant even over the air.

Alone among these poems "La Faux relevée" ("The Scythe
Lifted Again") seems to combine, in what might be, from its tone,
a sixteenth-century text, all the elements within a majestic scope.
The poet's fate is likened to that of the fountain, with whose generosity he has often been identified; we quote the lines again, as
befits the outflowing: "Fontaine, qui tremblez dans votre étroit
réduit,/Mon gain, aux soifs des champs, vous le prodiguerez"
("Fountain, trembling within your narrow nook,/My gain you'll
spread bounteous to the fields athirst") (LM, 184). The field of the
poem also is clearly stretched out, from the narrow to the broad,
from the wet to the fiery, "de l'humide fougère au mimosa
fiévreux" ("from humid fern to fevered mimosa"). This is the
privileged space of love as of poetry, outside of which the land is
devastated: "Le mouvement d'aimer, s'abaissant, vous dira:/
'Hormis là, nul endroit, la disgrâce est partout' " ("The motion of
loving, bending down, will tell you:/'Apart from there, nowhere,
disgrace is on all sides' "). Now over the land to be harvested,
which has been first redeemed, the menace is lifted: to the vertical-
ity of the verb "lifted again" the verb "bending down" responds
("relevée ... s'abaissant"), as love responds to the threat of death.
This poem, while in a sense placed also "above the wind" by its

cosmic scope — for the scythe will cut each of us down forever — has a depth to its sentiment and an inescapable drive to its images, and a range of meaning befitting its position near the end of its series and of *Les Matinaux*.

G. Quitter (To Leave)

The last series in the volume contains a picture quite simply entitled "L'Allégresse" ("Gladness"), showing the imbrication of one element into another, so that images of air are inseparable from those of water, the formal factors being arranged in what would in poetry be called "embraced rhymes" (*a b b a*): "Les nuages sont dans les rivières, les torrents parcourent le ciel" ("Clouds are in the rivers, torrents course through the sky") (LM, 205). Here with the element of air, all other factors are at last combined, so that wheat and harvest, hunger and plenty converge: "Le temps de la famine et celui de la moisson, l'un sous l'autre dans l'air haillonneux, ont effacé leur différence" ("The time of famine and the time of harvest, one beneath the other in the tattered air, have wiped out their difference"). All the images of transition subside, together with those of obscurity, for in the expression "Il n'y a plus de seuil aux maisons, de fumée aux clairières" ("No more threshold to the houses, nor smoke to the clearings"), the word "Claire" resounds, reminding us of the play "Claire," from the year 1949 (to be discussed later in this book). Transparency is thus allied to freshness once more, and all factors and elements culminate in the mood of joy which is the mood of this text, and of which, perhaps, the convergence of air, earth, fire, and water is the most profound representation, like an integrity found, at least temporarily.

IV   Le Nu perdu (Nakedness Lost)

The entire volume could be placed under the title of its first collection, *Retour amont,* for its carefully structured progress leads, in fact, upland, from the initial images of fire and water — "Le bûcher a fondu la neige" ("The fire has melted the snow") (NP, 14) — to the final text of *Contre une maison sèche* with its four elements whose convergence is called "a simplicity": "Le feu monte, la terre emprunte, la neige vole..." ("Fire is rising, earth borrowing, snow flying...") ([JG] NP, 131). The dry house on which all the poems lean and, at the same time, in opposition to which they construct themselves — that is, the two senses of the word "against" or "contre" — is at once a mountain, supporting their slow ascent, and a tomb whose sterility is redeemed by the flow of their words, alone capable of overcoming the dryness of "maison sèche." The titles themselves are indicative of the elements presently under discussion, for the upland of "retour amont" is clearly based on both the elements of earth and of water, "amont" meaning "upstream" and also the steep and arid side of a mountain.

The description of *L'Effroi la joie* (*The Dread the Joy*) given at the outset is dependent on the night air with its stars:

Enchemisé dans les violences de sa nuit, le corps de notre vie est pointillé d'une infinité de parcelles lumineuses coûteuses. Ah! quel sérail.

Robed in the violence of its night, the body of our life is dotted with an infinity of costly luminous particles. Ah! what a seraglio. (NP, 101)

The poem serves as the double of the preceding collection, *Le Chien de coeur* (*Dog of the Heart*), which conveys the climate of the poet's sudden malady on May 3, 1968:

...la foudre que j'avais si souvent regardée avec envie dans le ciel éclata dans ma tête, m'offrant sur un fond de ténèbres propres à moi le visage aérien de l'éclair emprunté à l'orage le plus matériel qui fût.

...the lightning I had so often observed enviously in the sky burst within my head, offering me against a ground of shadows all my own, the aerial aspect of the flash borrowed from the most material storm possible. (NP, 87)

Both texts imply the merging of lightning and of stars, stressing again the vertical movement of the language itself, upstream against the current. The movement is stressed still more in Char's last texts, *Aromates chasseurs,* based on the figure of Orion the giant, the hunter, and finally, the constellation.

A. Retour amont (Return Upland)

As in all dry lands, there is a special value attached to water in the Vaucluse. Partly for that reason, perhaps, the shift from the physical to the metaphorical is more easily made in these poems by

the means of water than by any other element. Even in the barest
description, a depth is generally sensed, of which one of the first
poems furnishes an excellent example. The opening line of the
poem "Couchés en terre de douleur" ("Bedded in a land of suffering") has an echo in snow-melting fire and in the line "L'eau glissa
bouillante au torrent" ("The water slid boiling to the torrent")
(NP, 12). Then the boiling water is echoed by the blood, both
images continued by the butcher's breathing in the second part of
the poem: the massacre of the heretical Vaudois at Merindol is thus
sketched out, with the trace of suffering exposed even under the
snow. From there to another kind of suffering, still represented by
water — an identification frequent with René Char — in the
following poem the reading moves easily. "Tracé sur le gouffre"
("Traced upon the Abyss") very briefly identifies the Sorgue in its
course between the mountains, in a closed valley which refers to the
Vaucluse (val clausa), with a human life in its quiet tragedy. We
quote the entire poem for its significance within the cycle:

Dans la plaie chimérique de Vaucluse je vous ai regardé souffrir. Là, bien
qu'abaissé, vous étiez une eau verte, et encore une route. Vous traversiez la
mort en son désordre. Fleur vallonnée d'un secret continu.

In the chimerical wound of Vaucluse I watched you suffering. There,
although subsided, you were a green water, and yet a road. You traversed
death in its disorder. Flower valleyed by a continuous secret. (NP, 14)

Some apparently more cheerful lines from another poem join these
in the same collection, much of which is "valleyed" by this
sadness:

> une vallée ouverte
>   une côte qui brille
> un sentier d'alliance
>   ont envahi la ville
> où la libre douleur est sous le vif de l'eau.

> an open valley
>   a gleaming coast
> a path of assent
>   have invaded the town
> where free pain is under the quick of the water.
>   ([JG] NP, 27)

All the linden branches of Buis-les-Baronnies, whose fragrance invades the town at festival time (whence the open invitation to the dance) cannot alter the suffering made still more vivid by the "quick" of the water. We think too of the poem "Aiguevive" ("Quick Water") ("eau vive") and of the springtime swell of the water, of those "eaux des mécénats printanniers" with their sense of a new beginning, after a suffering long endured.

As each poem deepens in rereading, and intensifies too the strength of the others, the image of a well dug profoundly into the earth conveys the risk of any profound feeling, and, at the same time, insists on its essential worth. In a poem dedicated to Yvonne Zervos and subtitled "La Soif hospitalière" ("Hospitable Thirst"), we read the quiet statement of an unusual love, already quoted: "Qui a creusé le puits et hisse l'eau gisante/Risque son coeur dans l'écart de ses mains" ("Whoever has dug the well and raises recumbent water/Risks his heart in the disjoining of his hands") ([JG] NP, 30). The well's image haunts much of this poetry, as the source of spiritual as well as material nourishment, and as the place of declaration and of healing. In this traditional spot, for instance, the unicorn — the image of the human spirit, according to the alchemists — rests from his fleeing, or a knight meets a maiden or laments his love. In the title poem of this collection, "Le Nu perdu," certain chosen beings are said to lift to the edge of the well the "flowering circle" of the bucket which will rally the others about them, regenerating life, as the dipping of the bucket in the well causes the ripples to blossom outward. These persons are kept naked by the very force of the wind, protected only by the softest covering of night while they accomplish the ritual gesture of redemption. Here the intensity of one element in its curative power seems to call forth another, as space and air answer the vitality of the quickened water.

Water serves as the communicating element, offering and linking certain privileged beings to others. In "Faction du muet" ("Sentinel of the Mute"), the poet speaks of joining his ageless violence and his mystery with the courage of a few persons and of shivering "comme une barque incontinente au-dessus des fonds cloisonnés" ("like an incontinent vessel above partitioned depths") (NP, 28). Now the myth of the hero who sets out to redeem a wasteland passes through these waters. All the different shapes and colors assumed, in Char's work, by the element of water over time, such as "the black waters of the word," the "water of white swamps," the long cutting reeds of a little stream, and the "green water" of the Sorgue join the depths here, each adding meaning to the others. All the network of images is aroused by even the simplest and briefest allusion, such as that of the abyss of suffering, like the river and the well. On the other hand, when all the four elements are included, there is not the same summoning of each to each.

"Effacement du peuplier" ("Effacing of a Poplar Tree") presents a storm and its raging wind swirling about the earth where a poplar grows. Each element is present, but none contributes to a further resonance, as if this were uniquely a poem of description. The poplar grows and watches over the great wind whose fierceness serves to sharpen its attention: the anthropomorphic attribution rings true in a poetry where the natural and the human are, always, so intimately linked.

Precisely the opposite tone rules in the next poem, "Chérir Thouzon" ("To Cherish Thouzon"), a poem not of nature as are most of the others discussed so far, but rather of human construction. Over the ruins of the castle at Thouzon, at dawn, a granite dove stretches his wings: the dove — here only half-visible — is a recognized symbol of the early Christian church. The black waters of night have withdrawn, flowing back over the humid slopes with their coursing foam. And as the moon, like a powder horn, mixes "the last blood and the first loam," in an alchemical combining of liquid and earth, there remains a "hope" of snow. One of the most understated and condensed poems of Char, this text is as strong in its visual as in its symbolic effect. The black waters, the white ocean foam, and the red blood contrast with the images of air and fog, the day with its white clouds circling over the ruins, and the pale moon at its work related to the tides and the earth, whose sign rules the last word of the poem: "the first loam."

The same sort of contrast, particularly prevalent in the poems of *Retour amont,* is visible in "Mirage des aiguilles" ("Mirage of the Peaks"), where fire displays a full metaphorical value: "Comment, faible écolier, convertir l'avenir et détiser ce feu tant questionné, tant remué, tombé sur ton regard fautif?" ("How may we, as a frail beginner, convert the future and rake out this fire interrogated and stirred up so often, which has caught your offending gaze?") (NP, 17). The testing place of fire is situated between a sea whose glaciers have been conquered by men, and a space where fire and wind hold sway.

"Aux portes d'Aerea" contrasts "la vivante nuit du ciel" with a rose in tears, opening in the present under the aim of an industrial or "iron" bee. Here the natural and therefore vivid sky of the past and lost city is supplanted by the menace of the present already too old, wounding the land of the lost city (supposed, by Pliny, to have been situated between Orange and Avignon). Again this nakedness has been lost, and cannot be recaptured, this simplicity of a past has been destroyed by the unnatural and can only be recreated in an artificiality which will not leave it intact. Space and sadness predominate.

In the poems following, for example, in "Devancier" ("Forerunner"), the poet will dig his tomb in the air, as the earth relinquishes its hold over the human, to fulfill a poet's fate. The same absolute contrast is shown in a poem written on the theme of a "village perché" or a town suspended in the air on a jutting rock, the "vertical village" of Venasque, whose church with its ancient baptismal font stands solid as if frozen under the mutinous cold, as Char describes the long winter winds, the mistral melancholy to ardent men: water and wind eventually triumph over fire, as the very brevity of the poem seems to indicate, making a harsh statement in a rocky setting. But toward the end of the collection, three poems in succession demonstrate the substantial strength of the opposition of elements to each other, a structure sufficient for the basis of each poem.

Each of the poems plays, like "Venasque," hot against cold, and is, like that poem, of a stark profile, as the titles indicate. "Deshérence" is a portrait of a poet exiled after his house is torn open, a disaster he compares to fire raging through an ancient night. Already, the visual contrast is as stark as, for instance, that of the candle flame against the darkness in "Servante" or the glowworm against the land of shadow in "Le Banc d'ocre" ("The Ochre Seam") as the bright/dark setting prepares the ground for the elemental oppositions in the poem. The poet, unlike other beings, whose presence therefore he threatens, is menaced like the wolf, to whose marginal condition he often compares his own — this poem should be juxtaposed with the extraordinary text called "Marmonnement" ("Mumbling"), where the convergence of poet and chased animal beyond the "living waters" explains the tone of many other poems. Here, the violence of the situation matches the violence of his characters: "Mon chagrin persistant/D'un nuage de neige/Obtient un lac de sang./Cruauté aime vivre" ("My persistent grief/Out of a snow cloud/Obtains a lake of blood./Cruelty likes to live") ([JG] NP, 44). The opposition of the two forms of the water to each other, not only cold to hot — where the lake of blood takes up Baudelaire's identical image in "La Cloche fêlée," another portrait of an anguished poet — but phonetically, as the repetition of the soft *g* in "nua*g*e de nei*g*e" sounds against the harshness of the "*l*ac de *s*ang" with its stop, its sibilant, and its nasal sound again used to stress, here accentuating the cruelty at once natural to the animal and forced upon him by society's rejection.

"Dernière marche" ("Last Step") moves in fact a step beyond "Déshérence" by its vertical progression in the direction we discussed in opening our essay on *Le Nu perdu* and to which we will return shortly in speaking of the poem of "upland":

> Moyeu de l'air fondamental
> Durcissant l'eau des blancs marais,
> Sans souffrir, enfin sans souffrance,
> Admis dans le verbe frileux,
> Je dirai: 'Monte' au cercle chaud.
>
> Hub of fundamental air
> Hardening the water of white swamps,
> Without suffering, finally without pain,
> Admitted to the chilly word,
> I shall say: "Climb" to the ardent circle.
> (NP, 45)

The cold air hardens the water, for here the "white swamps" resemble the "cloud of snow" in the preceding poem, marking the unforgiving chill of the poetic word into which now the difficult poet has been accepted, after his erstwhile marginal situation. In poetic opposition, the sun rises, and its hot circle ends the passage.

The third poem is the final step of this trilogy, if we may apply the term to the three steps advancing from disinheritance to the "end of solemnities" as three possible answers to the image of the house by means of which the situation of the poet is described. Here he deliberately takes his fire within his dwelling as an opposition to the wet of the storm outside, and to the "frost" of passers-by. But, and this is a fitting end to the triple statement of these

poems, this solitary fire does not finally suffice for the poet's feeling of responsibility, and as the "white flame" expires, he leaves
the walls of the house for the storm, unprotected like the exiled
wolf, but free from custom, as are all self-chosen marginal beings:
"Sans solennité je franchis ce monde muré: j'aimerai sans manteau
ce qui tremblait sous moi" ("Without ceremony, I step across this
walled-up world: I shall love uncloaked what was trembling under
me") (NP, 46). The relation of the initial withdrawal and self-
protection, "Je rentrai le feu dans la maison" ("I brought the fire
into the house"), to the final going forth makes a metaphorical
extension of the ambiguous contrast between fire and water or the
heat and cold of the world. The same moment informs the spirit of
La Nuit talismanique in whose dreaming the flame of one candle
within balances the storm outside: the quiet dwelling of a poet and
an interior lighting on one hand and, on the other, the raging of
"the gods of old" and exterior spectacle.

Thus the simplest analysis of opposition in the physical realm of
elements in all three poems, fire against water, for instance, can
situate a poet's project in general. Different readings will discover
different paths, and any of them might take another at another
time: one characteristic of great poetry is its reach, sufficient for
any number of paths.

To close the description of this major collection, let us look at the
texts associated with the upland, each one specifically signaled by
the word "amont."

The ascent upland or upstream, for the *Retour amont* inscribed
thus under the signs both of earth and water, by the deliberate
ambiguity of a single word, becomes markedly steep at the poem
called "Aiguevive" ("Quickwater"), whose title has already been
discussed. The texts are divided in two paragraphs, for a double
moment. The first begins with "La reculée aux sources," a return
to the origin of the waters, and the second balances it with "Revers
des sources": "Pays d'amont, pays sans biens, hôte pelé, je roule
ma chance vers vous" ("land of upstream, land without riches,
host stripped bare, I roll my fortune toward you") ([JG] NP, 35). To
stake one's luck on the poorest land is a choice more poetic than
practical, made here in full consciousness of the difficulty and in
the love of risk. At the conclusion of the poem "la faute est levée"
("transgression is removed"); without wishing to penetrate the
mystery of the fault or of that redemption, the reader is neverthe-

less conscious of the metaphorical correspondence between the moral lifting of the blame and the rise upland.

The title of the next poem we might read, "Le Village vertical," situates the text in a standing position, appropriate to a poem of expectation, surrounded by all the "amplitude d'amont" (NP, 36). But the lightning flash is said to join the ordinary noise of human life to the valued silence of the mountain, as a needle joins two fabrics: the end of the poem finds the sharpest form possible, the dart of light whose intensity is mirrored in the single last word, as fiery in its three syllables as the flash it represents: "Le dard qui liait les deux draps/Vie contre vie, clameur et mont,/Fulgura" ("The dart joining both sheets together,/Life against life, clamor and mountain,/Flashed") ([JG] NP, 36). The delicate aim of the flash contrasts with the wide backdrop of the land in its vast expanse, as the fire plays against the earth, and the last lines of the poem against the others. Both the "retour amont" and the "amplitude d'amont," are finally subsumed under the element of fire.

A prose text explains the line of human progress, seen in three stages, as the poems of upland are three: "Notre figure terrestre n'est que le second tiers d'une poursuite continue, un point, amont" ("Our earthly face is only the second half of a continuous pursuit, a point, upland") (NP, 38). The rising perspective granted, as the reader climbs upward with the poet, prepares the way for the final poem of the collection, "L'Ouest derrière soi perdu" ("The West Lost behind You"), a brief, radiant text, including all the elements as seen from the summit:

Le point fond, Les sources versent. Amont éclate. Et en bas le delta verdit. Le chant des frontières s'étend jusqu'au belvédère d'aval. Content de peu est le pollen des aulnes.

. . . .

The point melts. The springs pour out. Upland bursts forth. And below, the delta turns green. The frontier song reaches to the vantage point of downstream. Easily contented is the alders' pollen. (NP, 48)

Thus an image of convergence is followed by a liquid abundance and a fiery vision of earth, lit by the sun, juxtaposing in a brief space all the substances on which our present study is based. The text ends joyfully, with the greening of a delta responding to and redeeming the "impracticable delta" in the poem "Aiguevive."

From a lookout over the path already traveled, comes a statement of natural acceptance, where the small must suffice. In a poem of 1972, from *La Nuit talismanique,* we will read: "Le roi des aulnes se meurt" ("The alder-king is dying") and that poem will then take on a singular resonance from the memory of these alders, for which a little was enough.

The collection *Retour amont* ends on this note of gladness, at the return upland to a country within a poetic mind. Char points out that these poems are arranged geographically, leading toward a mountain — but it is clear that the mountain is finally interior, as was the path.

B. Dans la pluie giboyeuse (In the Quarried Rain)

The title *Dans la pluie giboyeuse* responds to the question asked in the first lines of the opening text: *"Where shall we spend our days* at present?" (NP, 51). The choice is between a destructive spirit ("among the incessant chopping of a hatchet gone mad") and this forest rain, where the vegetation left whole protects life of many kinds. It is to the latter, Char suggests, that we should wed our own breath, offering to the storm and its *"confused fertility, these powerful warring opposites, that, drinking at swollen springs they may fuse in an inexplicable loam."* So the entire collection is destined to the mingling of elements: air with water, or breath with storm, oppositions dissolving together, as if by the renewal of a springtime flow, into a fertile earth. Even a "petite pluie réjouit le feuillage" ("a small rain makes the foliage rejoice") (NP, 55), as one of these texts reads. Water is favorable to growth and is a source of happiness; deprived of its foliage, on the other hand, by times of dryness and destitution, such as those the hatchet threatens, the land is defeated: "Dépouillée, la terre plia" ("Stripped, the land capitulated") (NP, 63).

The theme runs through to the final texts of the collection, where, in rapid succession, four terse poems deal with the renewing power of water, for the earth and for man. Two pairs face each other, as in the title "Redoublement" ("Doubling"), a term which indicates, in our reading, the increase of each text by its facing text, as if two mirrors reflected a double image. The poem by that name describes an endless beach with endless waves bringing up pebbles, that is, a renewing image to which the falling rain offers its own ceaselessness: "Et la pluie apeurée faisant pont, pour ne pas apaiser" ("And the timorous rain making a bridge, so as not to appease") (NP, 80). Facing this endless stretch imagined is another description of rain, falling in one long sentence on what is called in the title a battered shelter ("L'Abri rudoyé") and then in one instant stopped short from its heavy splattering:

De tout temps j'ai aimé sur un chemin de terre la proximité d'un filet d'eau tombé du ciel qui vient et va se chassant seul et la tendre gaucherie de l'herbe médiane qu'une charge de pierres arrête comme un revers obscur met fin à la pensée.

From all time I have loved on a dirt path the nearness of a trickle of water fallen from the sky which comes and goes pursuing itself alone and the tender awkwardness of the median grass which a flurry of stones stops as an obscure reversal puts an end to thought. (NP, 81)

The final texts, "Permanent invisible" ("Enduring Invisible") and "Ni éternel ni temporel" ("Neither Eternal nor Temporal"), are both inscribed under the sign of time, as if the joined title of the diptych were to read: neither eternal nor temporal but rather enduring. In the first of the two, the "gibier," the prey of the prey-filled rain in the collection's title, returns: "O mon distant gibier la nuit où je m'abaisse/Pour un novice corps à corps./Boire frileusement, être brutal répare" ("Oh my far-off prey the night where I stoop/For a novice wrestling./To drink shivering, to be brutal restores you") (NP, 82). The hunt's brutality is itself as restorative as drinking from a deep and chilly well: here we remember the water lifted from the well of "Yvonne: la soif hospitalière" and its redemptive power which is echoed in the last text here, where the green wheat of springtime is "quenched with water on its luminous color" (NP, 83), as if its nutritive essence were to be increased by a miraculous moisture.

This collection then begins and ends in nourishment, as opposed to destruction, in joining as opposed to separation, but also in action as opposed to passivity: the hunt is linked, elsewhere, to the myth of the unicorn and of the poet, both chased and chasing, both reposing, at moments, by a well whose waters are said to cure.

As for the joining of enemy terms, the second poem's title continues the theme. "D'un même lien" ("With One and the Same Bond"), it reads, and in it, as in the prose text following it, the elements merge: matinal brightness in a meadow, flames and fire, dew and rain, compared to the natural alternations of sun and moon, or the rhythmical alternations of brake and whip, all arranged "in a hallucinatory order." Logic is banished from the instinctive reactions of man to the cycles of the world he inhabits. More than in any preceding collection, each element is here given its unique place, more clearly defined than before. In order of appearance, then, in "Possessions extérieures" ("Exterior Possessions"), our dreams are linked to the "infinite of the sky" in its writing, by means of the stars, which we interpret in accord with our own dreams. The value given to the element of air is again the essential one,[16] and more than ever is placed in an intimate correspondence with the essential significance of fire, enduring from this time through *La Nuit talismanique.*

Here a general remark can be made: as air represents the exterior relation of our imagination to the universe, so the candlelight, which will be the guiding image of *La Nuit talismanique,* represents the interior: again we think of Bachelard's *L'Air et les songes* (*Air and Dreams*) on one hand and, on the other, of the continuity of his thought from his early *La Psychanalyse du feu* (*The Psychoanalysis of Fire*) to *La Flamme d'une chandelle* (*The Flame of a Candle*), written toward the end of his life. The enemy terms are undeniably complementary, and the double universe in which Char dwells is reflected in the couple of facing poems.

The double poem called "Sur un même axe" ("On the Same Axis") is composed of what one might call an interior part and an exterior one, written a month later. The former, "Justesse de Georges de La Tour," opens with an invocation to a flame. "The unique condition for not retreating forever was to enter the circle of the candle, to remain in it, not yielding to the temptation of replacing the shadows by the dawn, and their fully nourished flash by an inconstant term" (NP, 73). La Tour's characteristic candlelight, seen sometimes as illuminating the faces grouped around it, or, in another canvas, as shining through the fingers of the girl holding the candle, is a perfect image of fire as Char conceives it most often, illuminating what we might call an interior picture, as Char's poems lead us up an interior mountain. This same candlelight will return most vividly in *La Nuit talismanique,* but the images of Georges de La Tour are visible in Char's texts over a long period. Already in his wartime journal, *Feuillets d'Hypnos,* he mentions that he has one of La Tour's canvases pinned to his wall, and later, La Tour is said to be one of the painters furnishing the "wool strands" for the poet's rocky nest of refuge and of enduring. The presence of this candleflame endures throughout Char's work.

Our reading returns, as Char does often, to the flame: it balances the outer spectacle and puts to the test, by its suggestion of profundity, our own action in the world. For the twin poem of the one devoted to La Tour, that is, "Ruine d'Albion," is written in protest against the atomic installations on the plateau of Albion in the Vaucluse, a defense of a *site* which cannot be ruined in its essence, for it is always removed from the world of everyday constructions, as in a metaphysical place. (Compare also Char's essay, "La Provence Point Oméga," already mentioned.) The relation of the two perspectives, outer and inner, is now clear. We have already seen how earth is, of all the elements, the one most quickly changed to a symbol: here the geographical place is easily transferred to a spiritual one, the latter sought after the destruction of the former. We might compare this text to the one on the lost city of Aerea, ("Aux portes d'Aerea") as the search for an interior site is paralleled by the hope of an exterior land which might symbolize a value now lost, yet perhaps some day to be recovered. Finally, on the Mont Ventoux, whose bold summit he used to liken to a mirror for eagles, whose slopes form the background for the play *Sur les hauteurs* (*On the Heights*), for some of the illustrations in *La Nuit talismanique,* and for the metaphorical scene of the poem "Marmonnement," the marginal poet and the marginal animal always in exile find a point of encounter beyond the "quick waters." So the interior site, marked by the candleflame of the preceding text, absorbing within it the value of this exterior earth, and the private space of the exterior air, will finally be triumphant over the ravages of time and of men.

In *La Nuit talismanique,* the candleflame will be opposed to the harshness of an electric lamp, too similar to daylight to encourage dreaming. The poem "Rémanence" ("Remanence"), still in the collection under discussion, presents another avatar of fire: a "high lamp and its radiance," shining above an old table laden with fruit, as if in a nostalgic childhood memory, transposed then, toward the end of the poem, into a star which came "too close" to earth and is therefore destined, says Char, to perish before the poet, whose destiny seems metaphysically situated in parallel to the heavens. The image of the star, of the constellation, will recur, whether as an indication of our dreaming, as in "Possessions extérieures," or as an image of the poet, as Orion or the poet descended to earth in "Evadé d'archipel" and then received on high, in "Réception d'Orion," both from *Aromates chasseurs* of 1975. The candleflame is the modest and domestic precursor of the more mysterious illumination of star and constellation.

Finally, the convergence of elements in the two poems following "Rémanence" acts as a brief résumé of the metaphysical extension prevalent from now on in Char's poetry. The title "Cours des argiles" ("Course of Clays") already joins the elements of water and earth in the substance of clay. The earth expects inspiration from elsewhere, and the "living waters" predicted by the poem "Aiguevive" are anxiously summoned:

> Vois bien, portier aigu, du matin au matin,
> Longues, lovant leur jet, les ronces frénétiques,
> La terre nous presser de son regard absent,
> La douleur s'engourdir, grillon au chant égal,
> Et un dieu ne saillir que pour gonfler la soif
> De ceux dont la parole aux eaux vives s'adresse....

> Watch, acute porter, morning to morning
> Long, coiling their jets, the frantic brambles,
> The land pressing us with its absent gaze,
> The ache growing numb, a cricket's level song,
> And a god springing only to swell the thirst
> Of those whose speech is addressed to living waters....
>   ([JG] NP, 77)

Here we think of the poem "Buveuse" ("Drinker"), and of Char's explanation of its title: it is a plant constantly absorbing water, a person always thirsty for drink, thus a Bacchante, or — through a metaphorical interpretation, he suggests — an appeal for water as a profound desire, akin to the search for poetry itself. Offering a glass of water may be an act of great profundity, as we remember from *Artine*. All the images of water in this collection, whose title situates all the poems under its sign, are closely intertwined, being linked also to the preceding images of offering, restoring, and suffering. The land and the spirit are watered, redeemed from dryness, and prepared for new action. In "Dyne," whose title indicates the energy of water and, by extension, of poetic action, human history is traced from cave man ("l'homme transpercé," the man pierced as with the horn of a prehistoric beast, his battle depicted on the Lascaux wall) to the man of the future, seen here as "making fire with truth," constructing a land befitting his nature, already washed and watered, and yet bare and open to possibility: "Ainsi atteindras-tu au pays lavé et désert de ton défi. Jusque-là, sans calendrier, tu l'édifieras" ("Thus will you attain the cleansed and desert country of your challenge. Until then, with no calendar, you will construct it") (NP, 78).

The distance between the poem "Recours au ruisseau," previously discussed, where the poet traces his town "on the surface of the current," to the dismay of the masons, and this poem, where the construction is situated in "immemorial sites" and outside of time, will be judged according to the interpretation of each reader. They might be considered as different stages of an interior return always directed toward the future and toward a future dwelling of the mind, further upstream and further upland. The elements are absorbed at last into a cosmic landscape befitting the gesture of creation always undertaken afresh, in a time over which the calendar holds no sway.

In *Le Chien de coeur,* italicized and therefore stressed, all the possible senses of the image of lightning are apparent: an extraordinary concentration of air, fire, and water in the storm's torment and then in the form closest to human interiority; as lightning combines air and fire, so blood combines fire and water. "Our storms are essential to us," Char says elsewhere in this volume (NP, 124). One of the lessons learned from this storm is that of the intimate connection between the human and the natural. In *Contre une maison sèche (Against a Dry House)*, from which there comes the remark on the storms and their necessity for each of us, we are shown the unique value of the most intense flash as it knits together all moments: "The lightning outlines the present, slashes its garden, chases, without assailing, its extension, will no more cease to appear than to have been" ([JG] NP, 128). Now the extraordinary movement in this night of lightning, which we have compared elsewhere to the night of Pascal's *Mémorial* ("Feu feu...")[17] shows also, like the flash of a privileged understanding, those true moments. Its presence is felt from then on, particularly in such titles as that of the next volume, implicitly inscribed under the sign of fire: *L'Effroi la joie.*

Now according to the alchemists the dog signifies the earthbound body, or even death, but at full moon the mad dog changes to a soaring eagle, a free spirit. Char often emphasizes the inseparability of past, present, and future, for he believes that if we fail to attach the past to the present, we are less intelligent as to future consequences and always uselessly nostalgic, and that the future is implied in the present, which itself covers all three stages. Thus the aphoristic statement, in a prose text called "Lenteur de l'avenir" ("Slowness of the Future"): "Our earthly face is only the second third of a continuous pursuit, a point, upland," where the upland has a temporal referent as well as a metaphysical one, representing a future time as well as a future space. A similar statement in *Aromates chasseurs* combines the three moments: "This century has determined the existence of our two immemorial spaces: the first, the intimate space where our imagination and our sentiments came into play; the second, circular space, that of the concrete world. . . . Is there a third space on the way, outside the trajectory of the two known ones?" (AC, 7).

C. L'Effroi la joie (The Dread the Joy)

The first text of the series, italicized, takes up a motif in turn from the preliminary text of *Le Chien de coeur,* where the flash of understanding occurs before the poet has been returned to the universe, his body scattered in the winds: here the violent luminosity of the stars echoes the violence of human suffering, intensifying it: *"Robed in the violence of its night, the body of our life is dotted with an infinity of costly luminous particles. Ah! what a seraglio"* (NP, 101). The final exclamation takes us back to the text commented on above, "Possessions extérieures," for by our dreams we possess the night and its stars, which become part of us as surely as the lightning is part of our blood and its rhythm, and as the myriad stars correspond to our separate candleflames, all this in an essential relation of fire, and liquid, of the air of the heavens and our earth.

It remains to link the understanding of these relations between elements and their representations to the fourth element. The tone has deliberate variations, so that matinal and tenebral aspects alternate in the overall profile: in the brief and very light final text explicitly called "Joie," as the initial text of *Le Chien de coeur* and *L'Effroi la joie* did not need to be explicitly entitled "L'Effroi," a calm natural scene replaces and responds to the violent nocturnal scene of the lightning flash:

Comme tendrement rit la terre quand la neige s'éveille sur elle! Jour sur jour, gisante embrassée, elle pleure et rit. Le feu qui la fuyait l'épouse, à peine a disparu la neige.

How tenderly the earth laughs when snow wakens upon her! Day after day, lying in its embrace, it weeps and laughs. Scarcely has the snow disappeared when the fire which formerly fled from her, weds her. (NP, 112)

The earth now receives water and fire in the guise of winter and summer, as it will finally receive the hero whose profile is sketched above. Orion is said — in a text of *Aromates chasseurs* called "Réception d'Orion" — to be scattered into particles, each a star; thus the constellation is the destiny of the poet who chooses this figure as his own.[18]

But we think also of the text in *Retour amont* called "Devancier" ("Forerunner"), where the poet digs into the air "ma tombe et mon retour" ("my tomb and my return") (NP, 70). For the return upland is not just upward to the air, but also, and more essentially, to a land within the poet himself. And in *Aromates chasseurs,* Orion, "Evadé d'archipel" as from a constellation of stars, and descended to earth, will once again rise to his constellation, from which, in the scope of poetry, earth and the margin of mystery surrounding the poet (as he dwells upon it) are not to be separated. They converge, as do the past, present, and future moments, in the space of the poetic imagination, always joining upland and upstream, even now.

D. Contre une maison sèche (Against a Dry House)

These texts are said to be leaning against a dry house — the Provençal "bories," stone constructions thought to be of the Ligurian epoch, their stones holding without mortar in a dry season. The dry house can also be seen as representing a tomb, against which the living poetic word protests and hopes to hold, or a mountain against which a poet might lean, and whose slope might be visible in his poems. The pages of the texts are themselves built in two levels, with an original statement and its examination in italics below, like an *exemplum* and its meditation, or like the two

levels of a house, or two shutters answering each other. Against the
wall of the house the words are reflected, says the poet, but little by
little the two levels converge; the next to last text explicitly states
that the house is lost to view and reflects no further words. These
are, as much as the poems of *Retour amont,* a return upland, and
when the dry house disappears, it is as if the mountain had moved
inside the poet's vision. The entire collection is placed under the
direction of one word, by the first commentary, concerning the line
"S'il te faut repartir, prends appui contre une maison sèche" ("If
you must set out again, prop yourself against a dry house") ([JG]
NP, 115). The commentary seems at first not to reply to the text at
all, and the way in which the two texts fit together becomes
apparent only gradually. *"Levé avant son sens, un mot nous
éveille, nous prodigue la clarté du jour, un mot qui n'a pas rêvé"*
(*"Risen before its meaning, a word wakes us, lavishes on us the
brightness of day, a word that has not dreamed"*) ([JG] NP, 33).
Now this word would differ for each poet and each reader; for
Char it might resemble the word *connaissance,* "knowledge."

Now this first text is already marked by an absence of liquid
images: the "dry house" is to be recognized by a tree whose own
fruits are said to quench its thirst. It is as if, in this country now
interior, the lack of the concrete or exterior elements did not
impede an interior progress. The house is dry, not thirsty; the tree
needs only what it produces, and in that there might be a lesson for
man. After the absence of water, the next two texts speak of the
presence of the other elements: "Espace couleur de pomme.
Espace, brûlant compotier" ("Space apple-colored. Space,
burning fruit-dish") ([JG] NP, 116). So reads the entire statement,
a complete if terse description of summer air, burned red by the
sun's fire. On the facing page, the next passage joins man to earth
by implication: *"La terre a des mains..."* (*"Earth has hands..."*)
([JG] NP, 117), as do the following texts — of the same tone as the
frequent laments for a land murdered and stripped by human
hands, for instance, "Ruine d'Albion." "Avenir déjà raturé!
Monde plaintif!" ("Future already deleted! Plaintive world!")
(NP, 119), and again: *"Sont venus des tranche-montagnes qui
n'ont que ce que leurs yeux saisissent pour eux. Individus prompts
à terroriser"* (*"There have come swaggerers who have only what
their eyes seize for them. Individuals all set to terrorize"*) ([JG] NP,
122).[19] To counter this destruction, against a nature properly

"enraged" (*enragée*), the poet warns us against our tendency to reduce the elements of our own measure: "N'émonde pas la flamme, n'écourte pas la braise en son printemps" ("Don't prune the flame, don't curtail the ember in its spring-time") ([JG] NP, 123). A phrase present in the first version, later suppressed, makes clear our responsibility to the time after ours, and the reasons for which we should not "prune" what seems to us excessive: the original manuscript reads: "Ordonne un peu de vie future là où tu n'es pas parvenu" ("Put in order a bit of future life where you have not yet arrived").

Then Char substitutes for that sentence a more literal explanation of the possible danger of human interference with nature: "Les migrations, par les nuits froides, ne s'arrêteraient pas à ta vue" ("The migrations, on cold nights, would not stop at the sight of you") ([JG] NP, 123). Still later — for the sentence is absent from the proofs of the text — he adds a positive statement to balance the negative warnings, and here two further elements enter the text, on a metaphorical level: "Nous éprouvons les insomnies du Niagara et cherchons des terres émues, des terres propres à émouvoir une nature à nouveau enragée" ("We are going through the insomnias of Niagara and searching for stirred lands, for lands fit to stir a nature once more enraged") ([JG] NP, 123). In the entire long poem, fire and earth, closely linked, are dominant, and the springtime presence of lightning recurs. The burning space at the poem's beginning, the most literal of the fire images here, and this metaphorical fire not to be reduced lead to a more human and interior light, useful in its turn to nature: *"Coeur luisant n'éclaire pas que sa propre nuit. Il redresse le peu agile épi"* (*"Shining heart lights more than its own night. It reerects the scarcely nimble wheat-ear"*) ([JG] NP, 126). The progress to the interior land is seen more and more clearly, even in relation to this element, until a statement on "the fundamental urn," in which the first sentence had originally the starkness of the text on which the collection ends; it read, before its alteration: "Tout paradis est, par avance, perdu" ("All paradise is, in advance, lost"). For this the poet substitutes the image of the burning urn, in relation to the lightning flash: both consume all that is not essential, merging past, present, and future: "L'éclair trace le présent, en balafre le jardin, poursuit, sans assaillir, son extension, ne cessera de paraître comme d'avoir été" (NP, 128).

As a résumé of all the fiery images in this collection, and in all the works up to this moment, including the early energetic flames and red-hot weapons of *Arsenal,* the strange consummation of *Artine,* and the alchemical fires of *Abondance viendra,* as well as the raging psychological anger of *Fureur et mystère,* the morning sunlight of *Les Matinaux,* and the lightning flash described in *Le Chien de coeur* and *L'Effroi la joie,* we read a very simple commentary toward the end of these texts: "Soleil jouvenceau, je te vois; mais là où tu n'es pas" ("Sun, lad, I see you; but where you no longer are") ([JG] NP, 129). The sun has moved inside, with the poet's return.

The next to last text takes up the first word which stirred the poet's imagination ("a word that has not dreamed"), what we might call a primary word. Formerly, it was a brief sentence on mystery and on knowing: "Qui croit renouvelable l'énigme, la devient. Escaladant librement l'érosion béante, tantôt lumineux, tantôt obscur, savoir sans fonder sa loi" ("Whoever believes the enigma renewable, becomes it. Now luminous, now dim, scaling freely the yawning erosion, to know without finding will be his law") ([JG] NP, 130). But — and here the intimate link of man and earth is made clearer than ever — in both the statement and the commentary, which now merges with it, the erosion of time, the wearing away of human strength is evoked, accepted, and then even chosen above any easier meditation: *"On doit sans cesse en revenir à l'érosion. La douleur contre la perfection"* (*"One has to return again and again to erosion. Suffering versus perfection"*) ([JG] NP, 130). With this text, the italicized commentary ceases its separate life. We read at the bottom of the page: "Ici le mur sollicité de la maison perdue de vue ne renvoie plus de mots clairvoyants" ("Here the house lost to view, its wall when hailed no longer sends back clairvoyant words") ([JG] NP, 130).

The final text of this collection and of the volume *Le Nu perdu,* joins, as if in another "burning fruit dish," the major themes considered in a convergence of all the elements. The text is greatly reworked, but in one of the first versions, the convergence appears as the opening line, as the first and clearest evidence: "Une simplicité s'ébauche: le feu monte, la terre emprunte, la neige vole, la rixe éclate" (NP, 130). Originally, this was followed by a restatement of the same motif as in the fruit bowl consuming and merging all things: "Aucun n'a son terme en l'autre" ("No one of them has its end in the other").[20] Even when that statement of unity disappears, the convergence remains clear. All fear is put aside in this final text, where the dry house has gone together with all external things. "Je vois un tigre. Il voit. 'Salut'" ("I see a tiger. He sees. 'Morning'") ([JG] NP, 131). The formerly menacing is no longer menacing, as the mint of Provence sees the birth of a man over which everything will triumph. These herbs, growing wild, lend their fragrance to the final version of the text, to which they are added relatively late. Here the central image of *Aromates chasseurs* already makes its appearance, that of the aromatic herbs on whose smoke poetry rises.

And then, in tne final version, a first paragraph, exactly reversing the process of the preceding versions, was added to the initial statement. It will be noticed that the sun here has gone one final step in metaphorical interiorization, becoming a hope — in fact, the only hope — and a prediction, in the face of that lost paradise and in the face of death:

Tout ce que nous accomplirons d'essentiel à partir d'aujourd'hui, nous l'accomplirons faute de mieux. Sans contentement ni désespoir. Pour seul soleil: le boeuf écorché de Rembrandt. Mais comment se résigner à la date et à l'odeur sur le gîte affichées, nous qui, sur l'heure, sommes intelligents jusqu'aux conséquences?

All we accomplish from today on, we shall accomplish for want of something better. Neither contentment nor despair. Our only sun: Rembrandt's flayed ox. But how resign ourselves to the date and the smell marked on the joint, we who at a crisis are intelligent even to foresight? ([JG] NP, 131)

For the sun seems to take on now the role of that word which awakened the poet and became his law: "to know." Knowledge of death and its moment does not, however, include resignation to the horrendous sight of our own rotting meat. The "gîte," or abode, is also the gîte ("loin") of beef, in a dreadful ambiguity, and here it has its sticker attached to it, like a definite category of value. While science dissects, poetry is meant to know the whole of things, not just the parts: as if we were to contemplate Rembrandt's picture of the anatomy lesson we must struggle to remember in a corpse the man it was. This "only sun of knowledge" cannot guarantee us any more than knowledge, cannot establish a foundation, as the

preceding skepticism makes clear. It has to suffice alone, aware of
the end, and "for want of anything better." One dry house forms
an exterior and visible starting point for an interior journey, leading finally to the tomb, another dry house against which we maintain our being, holding to our single sun of knowledge, however
grim.

V   La Nuit talismanique (Talismanic Night)

"We must take away the earth from the four elements; it is only
the mirthful product of the three others" (NT, 69). Only night
"quenches and irrigates," says Char in this book of double inspiration, in which the drawings nourish the texts and vice versa, like
André Breton's image of the communicating vessels, whose con-
tents flow into one another, the image taken from the scientific
experiment of the same name. Dream and day are interwoven, and,
for Char, night and its liquid imagination and the reverie by a
candleflame give substance to eath other, like water and a modest
and humanized fire. The candle marks the space set apart for
meditation, complementary to the water of dream. If we follow the
distinction drawn by Bachelard between nighttime dreaming —
which he compares to a straight line, related to the masculine spirit
or "animus," and daytime reverie, in the form of a star, about
whose central focus different inspirations radiate — thus, a feminine sensitivity, inscribed under the figure of "anima," then the
texts of *La Nuit talismanique* are those of reverie rather than those
of dream. Their provenance remains mysterious. Char says of
them: "Another hand protects the flame," without specifying the
inspiration. "Servant or mistress, the breath and the hand, razing
and bruised, this flame which I need was lent to me by a candle,
mobile like the gaze. The nocturnal water poured out into the
greening circle of young brightness, making me night myself, while
the work streaking by set itself free" (NT, 12). This *"oeuvre
filante,"* streaking by as in a meteor's path, moves from the fire of
Le Marteau sans maître to this candleflame of a text whose proper
title reads: *La Nuit talismanique qui brillait dans son cercle* (*The
Talismanic Night Which Shone In Its Circle*). It completes, says the
poet, the "solitary gesture of raising a candle." The mystery of the
hand holding the flame is illustrative of the ambiguity on which
poetry flourishes.

And indeed the volume is situated on the other side of the clarity visible in *Les Matinaux;* its tone is quiet as if with a shadow which the light of day might undo. The first text following the preface contains, in a series of nocturnal meditations, eight brief poems from 1954 and then a series from almost twenty years later; the moments reflect upon each other, and are mutually nourishing, like the illustrations and the texts, or like those sets of double poems situated "on the same axis" which take their source from the same feeling and find their place at the same site, facing each to each. The three main themes appearing in the text of introduction all serve in a different way as meditations: on the night as a major source for the imagination, on the value of mystery, related to that same obscurity, and on its utility for a future as for all present moments of a life whose current is made more profound by the oneiric imagination in its flow:

La nuit porte nourriture, le soleil affine la partie nourrie.
Dans la nuit se tiennent nos apprentissages en état de servir à d'autres, après nous. Fertile est la fraîcheur de cette gardienne!
. . . .
Il ne fallait pas embraser le coeur de la nuit. Il fallait que l'obscur fût maître où se cisèle la rosée du matin.

Night brings nourishment, sun refines the part nourished.
By night our apprenticeships hold themselves ready to serve others, after us. Fertile is this guardian's coolness.
. . . .
It was wrong to fire the heart of night. It was fitting that the dark be master where the morning dew is carved. ([JG] NT, 15–16)

The candle has always kept its watch over the poet's insomnia (to which he was particularly prone in the years 1955–1958): so all the illustrations of the preceding texts inserted in the volume (Part I) could be inscribed under the double heading of fire and nocturnal water. The response of almost twenty years later, from 1972 (Part II), is at once the answer of candle to candle, of talisman to text, and of illustration to the thought it deepens. Many of these texts are punctuated by nocturnal motifs, and the image within the poem serves as a verbal equivalent of the illustration. Meditations on dreams and on our feeble control over them (a theme expressed in

"Possessions extérieures") dominate at first glance, and we remember the question "How to bring back to the bindweed of breath the indescribable hemorrhage?" (NT, 58). Here we think of all the images of breath and energy in *Arsenal* and also of the candle "close to our breath" in the text just quoted and of the strength of human passion, expressed through another element: "the earth where we desire is not the one which buries us. The hammer which affirms it does not have a crepuscular blow." And from *Le Marteau sans maître,* this optimistic assertion echoes throughout the length of that work. Then those examples of air and earth are joined with water still under the guise of night and the fire of sterile winds continues the motif of human breath: "Freedom is born at night, no matter where, in a chink of the wall, on the passing of glacial winds" (NT, 59). From the natural to the human, or from the concrete to the metaphoric, this text makes a gradual ascension: "A certain gaze of the earth brings into the world life-giving shrubs, at the most enflamed point. And we too, reciprocally.... Oh, my smallest smoke lifting over each true fire, we who are the contemporaries and the cloud of those who love us!" (NT, 60). For that conjunction of elements, of earth and fire and then of air and fire respectively, is, like any conjunction in Char's universe, oriented toward the moral.

The lessons his poetry is ready to teach are presented with a natural generosity which rarely separates poetry from nature, the natural from the human. Consider, for example, a statement which does not only concern its most evident subject: "Trees do not question each other, but if they are too close together, they make the gesture of avoiding each other" (NT, 62), and, from the following text: "The water of my land would run off more easily if it would go at a walking pace" (NT, 65). Char, speaking a simple thing, is speaking usually also of something greater.

The texts of Part II answer the texts of Part I as all these poems of 1972 answer those earlier ones, presented at the beginning. We read at the end of the first part, "Who is calling still...?," and the first title of the second part reads: "Each one is calling." Just so, all Char's texts are multiple, each summons the others, and all are directed toward many outcomes. Under the title of multiplicity, just quoted, the text begins by a description of the April mistral and the suffering such a wind provokes; it ends by an invocation to night, which we continue to identify with water, according to the poet's indications: "Night whose body has no bones, you alone should be still recognized as innocent" (NT, 78). The relation between mistral and liquid night, between suffering and innocence is made sufficiently clear, without a violation of what Char sees as the essential mystery of poetry.

The one text in this collection which most perfectly presents the value of the talismanic night is entitled: "Éclore en hiver" ("To Blossom in Winter"), a title whose moral lesson is given by its image: since the surrounding dark is propitious for meditation, the poet works not by a harsh electric light, but rather by the candle-flame: its "greening circle" then blossoms in winter as does the poetic imagination at night. *La Nuit talismanique* is not, strictly speaking, a "deeper" text than *Les Matinaux,* but its value is different, its days measured by a different calendar. Here the division of moments is not felt, supporting the previous identification of the nocturnal with the liquid or the flowing, with that which has neither bones nor hardness: "As night asserted itself...." From the candleflame, the poet learns to bend over and to look closely — as we have already, at this same text — "to see, nearing, a shadow giving birth to a shadow through the slant of a luminous shaft, and to scrutinize it" (NT, 87). In this close attention paid to the birth of shadows or to the birth of a poem, to the amount of shadow necessary to the latter, we see one lesson, and perhaps the most essential one, of the talismanic night. To render to night its innocence is to maintain its reserve: "how to render to man the night of his dreaming?" This entire volume is the appropriate answer to that one question posed in *Le Nu perdu.* Volume answers volume in Char's work, and differently, each time we look.

It should be said here, and in particular reference to *La Nuit talismanique,* that in his use of the imagery of water and fire, Char is remarkably close to the English metaphysical poets and their intense meditation of contrary elements, in particular of fire and water: his *emblems* may not always appear identical with those in the emblem books which inspired them, but his *talismans* include their shadow, as the flayed ox of Rembrandt also refers to a bleeding, or flaming heart, and the candle of *La Nuit talismanique* is itself aflame. Robert Peterson points out in his *Art of Ecstasy: Teresa, Bernini, and Crashaw*[21] (New York: Atheneum, 1972) the overwhelming importance of water for Saint Teresa and for every Castilian. The four stages he sketches in the meditation of water are in correspondence with Char's own water imagery in its relation to love and suffering, to ardor, and to nourishment. First, the water carried from the well: we think of the poem "Le Nu perdu," where the well's ripples are seen moving outward from the bucket as it dips up the water. Second, a larger quantity of water is taken with the waterwheel or a bucket and windlass: the former image haunts Char's imagination, like the waterwheels in the local river of the Sorgue, which then become, by a poetic transformation, "sun wheels," as the sun shines upon the dazzling white of the water turning in the air. Third, water flows from a stream or a brook: see "Recours au ruisseau," with its construction and reconstruction of a poetic dwelling, like the poem grappling with its own metaphysical destiny. Fourth and finally, the rain falling on a dry earth, like that of the Vaucluse: see the collection *Dans la pluie giboyeuse,* and in particular, "Redoublement," where the one line of the poem itself falls heavy and long, like a verbal weight.

Now the play of water against flame is as unmistakable in Saint Teresa's meditations as in that of all the metaphysical poets: the soul is described as issuing forth from itself as by a burning, becoming wholly flame, while this experience is closely linked with all the forms of water and its nourishing of ecstasy, with the erotic as with the religious. In Char's beautiful and brief text in honor of Georges de La Tour's "Madeleine à la veilleuse," the candleflame lighting the hand, the skull, and the poem as well as the canvas, is placed in vivid contrast with the implicit tears of remorse shed by the repentant Magdalene. A sensitive reading will contemplate the implied juxtaposition of tears and flame in "Madeleine à la veilleuse" while remembering the single glass of water in Char's early work *Artine,* a text of burning and of dreaming, and lastly with the candle lighting *La Nuit talismanique* and its coveted river of sleep. But in the present context the following passage from Tesauro on the Magdalene's eyes is particularly revealing: "What is this prodigy? Water and Flame, once bitter rivals, are now reconciled like peaceful bedfellows in Magdalene's eyes. . . . You will find in them a spring and a torch, you will draw fire from the water, water from the fire. Her eyes repeat the fabulous miracle of Mount Etna on whose top the snow is espoused to the fire. . . ."[22] (Many more of Char's images are "in proximity" with those of the metaphysical poets, for instance, with those of the *Silex Scintillans* — title of a collection by Thomas Vaughan — as in the line from "Le

Visage nuptial'': "Le silex frissonnait sous les sarments de l'espace'' ("The flint was trembling under the vine-shoots of space''). Or again, the wounding as if by a dart, not only for Saint Teresa, but also for each one chosen by and for love as in Crashaw's "Wishes'': "A well tam'd heart/For whose more noble smart/Love may bee long chusing a dart.'' The dart is at the same time a sting, and the bee and honey so omnipresent in Char's most recent poetry open the way to a series of interconnected images, to the hunter blinded by the beams of a flower's beauty as if by the bees, gathering the honey of a spirituality among the fragrance of some aromatic herbs, in whose presence the hunter is also hunted: Crashaw's bees swarm about the Name of Jesus:

> O they are wise:
> And know what *Sweetes* are suck't from out it.
> It is the Hive,
> By which they thrive,
> Where all their Hoard of Hony leyes.

All the corresponding images form, in a figurative sense, the flint from which the fire of the most condensed poems is struck, all the more intense for its reference to another time and place, haunting the poet's memory, and our own.

VI   Aromates chasseurs

In the title poem of this volume, the sorrow is silent, under the water: "Je voudrais que mon chagrin si vieux soit comme le gravier dans la rivière: tout au fond. Mes courants n'en auraient pas souci'' ("I would like my grief — so old it is — to be like the gravel in the river: at the very bottom. My currents would not care about it'') (AC, 12). Whereas, in the same poem, the role of fire is to liberate the storm, by a sensual lightning, so that we are nourished by the water, as it is lifted from the well and dances its pleasure at its dip of the bucket.

All these relationships reinforce each other, as do the references to another epoch. But of all the recent poems, "Note sibérienne'' is perhaps the most significant for our study. The "note'' is a cold one initially: snow is no longer carried by the hands of children, but is born and gathered up on the poet's face itself, in this "night increasingly more exiguous." And in direct opposition to this first paragraph of cold,the second is consecrated to fire:

Pourquoi alors cette répétition: nous sommes une étincelle à l'origine inconnue qui incendions toujours plus avant. Ce feu, nous l'entendons râler et crier, à l'instant d'être consumés? Rien, sinon que nous étions souffrants, au point que le vaste silence, en son centre, se brisait.
. . . .

Why then this repetition: we are a spark of unknown origin, still burning further forward. Do we hear this fire agonizing and shouting, at the instant that we are consumed? Nothing, except that we were suffering, so much so that the vast silence, in its center, was breaking. (AC, 34)

In this extraordinary text, against the snow, the ardor of a poet's progress is traced, in pain and to the extent of rupturing the precious silence, intact until then. This text should be placed alongside the last part of *Contre une maison sèche* which itself goes past ordinary bounds of optimism and pessimism to a simply stated acceptance of despair: "for want of anything better," and compared too with "Tracé sur le gouffre," with its river of pain hollowing out the Vaucluse. There voice and silence take on their true value under the currents, deeper than sound, as here the quiet — whose worth has been stressed in the text first considered — breaks for one voiceless cry. One has only to compare these three texts with the tongue of the ox giving its death rattle at the center of the last text of *Abondance viendra* ("la lave") to see the distance the poet has led us, from horror outspoken to the restraint of a "nordic countenance" at the center of this text.

To recapitulate the pillars, first to last, is unnecessary. But each of the four Orion poems could be seen as having an apparent source in one of the elements, and manages to link all to all in turn. Orion escapes to satisfy his "earthly" thirst — that desire Char always associates with water, as in "Buveuse" — whereas in the matching poem "Réception d'Orion," the human meteor has the whole earth for honey, and is thus materially associated with that element. In his ascent toward the stars which he chases and whose fiery radiance blinds him, he prepares a double way both for the poems of loftiness and air; — "Orion Iroquois" or the "highsteel" worker, constructor of the giant bridges in the sky, — and for the final poem, which combines all the elements. Orion sits now on the earth, by the river, remembering a fire of fury and mystery and rebellion, and then departs toward a star, a flame localized in the air, from which originally he came and to which he returns, in a reverse Promethean gesture, or a *Retour amont,* taking the moral "relit metal" of human courage to the immaterial flame of a star. This text corresponds to *L'Anneau de la licorne* (*"The Ring of the Unicorn"*), where the poet is apart, in *La Nuit talismanique,* at the edge of a constellation — as the unicorn signifies the spirit, so, in that text and in this one, the spirit is alone in its journey and in its dwelling.

Here, at the conclusion of this study of the elements and of the poem, it is perhaps necessary to bear in mind the two basic convictions on which it is based. First, that the essential — and fortunate — subjectivity of each reading is situated in time and always subject to reevaluation. And second, that the infinite space of great poetry can be seen through any of a number of windows — no matter how narrow in appearance — each opening out upon it.

CHAPTER 5

Theater for a Clear Season

BETWEEN 1946 and 1952, Char wrote a series of works for a "seasonal theater," three plays and three ballets, one of which is called "a sedition"; all are seditious, in a sense which should become clear in our discussion. All these works are gathered in a volume entitled *Trois Coups sous les arbres,* which is to say: the three knocks that signal the beginning of a theatrical spectacle ("les trois coups") but sounding under trees. These are all outside presentations as opposed to inside ones. They are intended for open spaces, not enclosed ones, are informal instead of formal, and — more significant still — are focused on landscape rather than on culture, maintaining themselves closer to nature and to the elements than to human architecture. "La poésie est de toutes les eaux celle qui s'attache le moins au reflet de ses ponts." "Poetry is of all waters the one lingering the least in the reflection of its bridges." (SP, 10)

As we would expect, then, the plays have neither the profound complexity nor the dense texture of Char's prose poems; they are all situated on the more approachable side of his mountainous temperament, if we are to follow the image he gives of its two slopes: the more abrupt and the easier. The collective volume is subtitled: *Théâtre saisonnier* (*Seasonal Theater*): this is plainly the theater of a summer, not intended for the rigors of winter, nor conducive to deep meditation.

Each piece has its own peculiar resonance, by which we mean both its tone and the echoes of that tone in the memory of the spectator or the reader. A brief description of each spectacle, arranged chronologically according to the genre: ballet or play, will show their common themes and images.

136

I   *Spectacles and Ballets*

Char's ballets almost resemble poems, in attitude and in form (containing, for instance, a prologue and several stanzas). In the general explanation Char gives of the last one, *La Conjuration,* we see why it is positioned at the conclusion of the volume, its significance thus underlined, and with it, that of all the ballets:

> *There are days when we dream of giving to our acts a less furtive meaning, when we turn, not in thoughtlessness, to our pride, so as to determine our priorities. . . .*
> *Before us, allusive dunes multiply their derision. Not the least alphabet for our love.*
> *How then should the dance not prevail as a remedy or simply as the fortuneteller of the unconscious and of tragedy? (Trois coups sous les arbres,* 245)[1]

Thus at the end of the book we are permitted to see the point of the spectacles: where words fall short ("not the least alphabet"), gesture sometimes suffices.

The first three spectacles or ballets are composed of gestures and limited commentary.

A. La Conjuration (The Conjuring)

A "solar smell of recently crushed wheat" and the loud chirping of crickets in the early twilight form the background for the ballet. A young man in red pants, and espadrilles, thin "as a cypress tree," his skin as reflective as a mirror, dances in a convulsion of repressed anguish, as if he were pitted against the countryside itself: "He tries to assault the landscape. We feel his fragility. He does not know his powers, his precise desires" (TC, 247). Furthermore, he appears insensitive: from among the birds flying in circles over his head, of which we see only the shadows, a swift falls to the ground at his feet. The dancer mimics the bird's distress, laughing while all the birds try to glimpse their reflection on his skin: he only opens and closes his arms like a fan, in an unfeeling gesture. We think here of Char's haunting poem on the swift, who falls from his joyous circling in the air above a house, because a thin gun is well-aimed. "Such is the heart," the poem concludes (FM, 214). The reader does not fail to link one bird to the other, one lack of feeling to the other, as if this spectacle were an epilogue to the poem.

The prologue presents a relatively enigmatic surface, conveying nevertheless a vague unrest. In the first "stanza" of the poem-ballet, dancing couples seek a glimpse of themselves in the man-who-mirrors, as the birds had, and this time he plays out his reflective role, although he will gradually show a certain tiredness and apprehension: "These beings have not yet been revealed to themselves. An extreme awkwardness, almost supplicating. Each tries to express himself according to his nature: exuberant, sly, generous, pathetic, stupid, etc." (TC, 248). The "interior image" of each appears; but one girl remains apart, dancing what Char calls "the dance of the magnet voluntarily depriving itself of its object." To combat her indifference, the central personage disguises himself as a worker, observes his new "obscurity" in a real mirror, then at noon goes to the square where the couples once more approach him, with curiosity and then hostility. The girl still dances a hermetic dance alone: "Dance of the kept secret and the raging spring. Dance of sublime independence" (TC, 250). Now "the man with mirroring skin" removes his obscuring garments and falls weakened at her feet, just as the swift in the prologue had fallen earlier — again we think of the line: "such is the heart." But the girl, insane, and nevertheless (or perhaps, therefore) in close contact with the universe, remains separate from human collectivity: now she dances "the gesture of the stars appearing and disappearing at night in the interstices of rapid clouds" (TC, 250).

In the last two stanzas, the man's natural authority over the others (symbolized in his power to reflect their inner selves) has disappeared, and he dances out his own tragedy, his disappointment in love. The description of his dance, as of the girl's, is the central focus of the ballet: "Farewell to the always fixed forms from which a lasting pleasure turns away.... THE FRUIT DOES NOT COME FROM THE FLOWER, IT IS ITS OPPOSITE. The fruit is the prolongation of evening. It is the hyphen between evening and risk. The flower limits itself to being only a diamond of daytime" (TC, 250–51). After this rather enigmatic commentary, the man hurls himself from the window.

A footnote of explanation reads: "The antinomy is insoluble. So the Man-Mirror, prince of knots, dies of error, pure from any compromise" (TC, 251). As he lies covered with mist at twilight, the dancers cluster around him once again imprisoned in their original misunderstanding of themselves without his reflection of their nature. The girl enters, dancing, with tenderness, intelligence, and passion, "the dance of the magnet about to apprehend its object." The mirror is dark, as the girl or the night itself — in its first and youngest form — takes final possession of his body. But just before the curtain falls in a "winged sound of a river flowing away," there appears a strange animal, said to be tracing out a pattern of tears, "cat or chimera? ... Who, except the one nourished on life, who provokes suffering, who perceives the ultimate sob, knows how the throat rips itself apart?" (TC, 251). This odd vision disappears before the triumph of night, but as its visibility fades here, the attentive reader might perhaps assimilate its figure to that of the suffering animal, slightly bleeding, in Artine's bed (1930), and, much later, to that distressed animal fleeing across the rocks in *La Nuit talismanique* (1972). There are many similar enigmatic presences in Char's universe, whose reappearance indicates their importance for him. They deepen the voluntary mystery, never to be completely effaced.

Similarly, the theme of clarity opposing darkness will reappear, even in the course of the other spectacles of this very seasonal theater, all of them traversed by the final sound of the river: if we were to continue our previous analysis of the elements, we would place this seasonal spectacle under the sign of water. It is often, as here, darkness which wins out over the brilliance of the mirror, the bright waters or the daily clarity. Given the preponderance of non-reflective images in Char's poems over the reflective ones, the conclusion is not surprising. For one stable and translucent poem in which a pink stream of water left after the rain sparkles ("The rosy face of the gully turns twice toward him the wave of its mirror," LM, 181), reflecting the narrator "such as he had dreamed himself to be," and one poem where birds regard themselves in the spring whose hostages they remain, are more than outweighed by many rapid poems of a water turning too quickly to reflect, of a water-wheel breaking up an iridescent surface into a white fury, or a rushing cascade, such as the Fontaine de Vaucluse in its springtime swell, and, on the other hand, a series of tragic and profound images, such as that of a greenish stream flowing like death, or of black waters of the word receding over the countryside, that of a well whose depths nourish but whose surface, disturbed by repeated dippings of the bucket — the ripples flowering outward — will not return reflections. Char's greatest poems are perhaps not the matinal ones, and they are rarely self-reflective. They are deep rather than sparkling, troubled as often as they are iridescent, seldom calm.

If we have given so much space to a work which is plainly not one of Char's major achievements, it is partly because of the triumph of night — see *La Nuit talismanique* — and partly because of the falling bird, whose image we have referred to. The dancer's physical agility had been stressed, as well as his *reflective* capacity, and the initial image of the bird falling betrayed the inconsistency of that agility and, as we see it now, of that capacity and clarity. The ballet is, after all, the tale of his capture by another force, by an obscurity opposite to his brightness as the female element is opposite to the male, the river opposite to the sun. Of course the capture fits in the natural cycle moving from day to night. The dancer's response to the bird's fall is a double one: first he collapses at the girl's feet, and finally he plunges from the window, while the spectacle is resolved by the fall of night. The wordplay, while not obtrusive, is none the less significant: "*la tombée* de la nuit" parallels the action of the man, as he falls (*il tombe*), in both of which there is the implicit echo of the grave, and thus of death (*la tombe*).

The title *La Conjuration* bears a slightly magical tone, characteristic also of the two other ballets; all three are far from the "realism" of Char's best-known play, *Le Soleil des eaux* (*The Sun of the Waters*). It is by their atmosphere and tone that they merit the title of poem-ballets.

B. L'Homme qui marchait dans un rayon de soleil
    (The Man Who Walked in a Shaft of Sunlight) (1949)

The spectacle is subtitled *Sedition in One Act,* and its introductory remarks already place it in the realm of an interior spectacle:

In the space of a head, which we could call, on this occasion, *theater,* there can be played the drama of *The Man Who Walked in a Shaft of Sunlight.* There is mud, mist, some saliva from a bad angel and a few patches of water shining under the spectators' seats. These latter don't know how they came in or how they will get out. The atmosphere is one of defiance and anguish, of embarrassment and of watchfulness, of an unknown but imminent fate (in the premonitions of some).

The theme of the work will probably not reach its distant resolution, or rather, it will bifurcate, summoned by some urgency which no one would have suspected. A head, even if it is alert, is the least certain theater there is. (TC, 227)

The action takes place as if it were under a moral judgment, with a jury acting as the guardian of a public duty, whom the person reminiscent of a Great Inquisitor ("Le Grand Audencier") sets against the audience, alongside the defendant: "the sentimental accomplices, the unknown friends of the one whom your verdict will soon affect . . . Their soul is attached to a particular justice, an enemy of yours" (TC, 232). But then, turning aside, he speaks in a fashion completely at odds with his previous manner, in lyric praise of rain, disquiet procured by water, of a Neptune who would have left the sea. (I will have occasion to comment later upon the interrelations of water imagery among the various dramatic works.)

Moreover, the subsequent action takes place under the rain, at four on an autumn afternoon, with every passerby dressed for the rain except a young man encircled by a light shaft, to the disbelief of those around him and of the jury. A girl passes, described as radiantly pale and bareheaded under the rain: "She is the attractive part of solitude, always loved in vain, the great Passerby . . ." (TC, 236). As the hero of the preceding ballet tried to engage the girl dancing apart in a game of reflection, here this equally strange personage tries to take the girl into his light ("He dances the hymn of sharing, the royal step of solar temptation"), while the jury continues to comment and to predict, like a modern substitute for the Greek chorus, and to mock: "It's too good! A saint losing his halo" (TC, 240). The dire predictions are justified, for he turns in anger against his imprisonment in his own bright circle, frees himself from it, and drops at the feet of the girl, as the Man-Mirror had done in the preceding ballet. She then dances "a dark circle" around him, as a reply to his luminous shaft now disappeared, and departs, to the mockery of the majority of jurors. While the twelfth juror eulogizes a "solitude always misunderstood," the rain continues to fall, closing off the spectacle in its own circular form, since it had opened by an invocation to the waters. As nightfall conquered clarity in *La Conjuration*, here the falling rain is victor even over one solitary sunbeam, the impractical and even impossible part of the landscape, which may have represented the unique element finally conquered. At the spectacle's conclusion, a mason building his construction in all serenity comments on a restless wind and on the coming night, which will be fearsome. (We think again of "Recours au ruisseau," where the poet builds his habitation further and further upstream, alarming the masons in their cautious competency.) Once again, the spectacle ends with the fall of the dark, visible in the preceding ballet, and here, only predicted. The ray of the marvelous has been extinguished, and no sharing between the brightness and the obscurity is proved possible.

C. L'Abominable des neiges (The Abominable Snowman)

The last on the list of characters is "The Himalayas constantly present." The principal personages are the first explorer, Docteur Hermez (as Hermes), and the Himalayan Venus or the abominable snowman, dressed as half-man, half-animal, in a fur which is then thrown off to reveal a young lady in a shiny bathing suit holding a poppy, with two small horns on her head, and accompanied by her satellite, in love with her and jealous of her affection for the explorer, who has had the courage to climb toward her planetary presence in the sky. With her fur cloak she protects the latter, who has fainted from the cold and fatigue, so that he may survive her departure for the heavens until his companions return him to the camp. But even as she shines brilliantly in the sky once more, the satellite, a young hunchback with a pure face, removes the fur and wears it, so that upon waking Hermez takes him for Venus, follows him over the side of an abyss and plunges to his death. Venus returns to condemn her satellite, dragging him after her forever in the sky, from which she will never again descend, as tragedy requires. Meanwhile, the explorers exult in having conquered Mount Everest. "So that there succeeds only what had been a limited material objective, while the hero succumbs, brought low by the intricacies of his sovereignty and his fate. ...Now that the Everest has been trampled, Venus will return to earth no more. From now on, the impossible is to be found in the human realm. What have we conquered, what have we won?" (TC, 35).

The entire spectacle is inscribed implicitly under the name of Venus ("Vénus victrix, Vénus d'Homère, Vénus himalayenne..." (TC, 33). Here she represents not only beauty, desire, and grace, but the spirit of the cold: "Beauty and snow in whom there are opposed and united limpidity and ambivalence, those conventionally inseparable qualities" (TC, 33). The conquering of Everest and the lessening of Venus's earthly power are intimately connected; when Venus returns to the sky, men have greater authority on earth; yet the whole tenor of the ballet seems to question whether this is really an advantage, as if some sort of beauty and mystery had been lost.

in the "progress" of human discovery. Similarly, *La Nuit talis-manique* ends with a warning, which, for being couched in modest and natural terms, is none the less grave: "Hirondelle, active ména-gère de la pointe des herbes, fouiller la rose, vois-tu, serait vanité des vanités" ("Swallow, active housekeeper of grass tips, to forage in the rose, don't you see, would be sheer foolishness") (NT, 95).

All three ballets thus turn about love, with a tragic ending, in the course of which the interaction between man and nature seems to be parallel. Night, sun, water, snow, mountains, play a role as great as that of any of the personages. The same will hold true of the plays next to be discussed.

II *Poetic Plays*

The plays seem more closely related to reality than the ballets; no hero clothed in sunbeams or in mirrorlike skins, no climbing of Mount Everest, no Venus descending from on high with her jealous satellite. The characters are, for the most part, recognizable local figures, and the tales have the feeling of everyday events.

The landscape is clearly that of the Vaucluse, centering around the river Sorgue in *Le Soleil des eaux,* and the Mont Ventoux in *Sur les hauteurs* (*On the Heights*). Claire could be any stream which converges with a larger one, but it is hard not to see it as the waters of the Sorgue also, eventually flowing into the Rhône. Each play is closely linked to its natural setting, which is of even greater impor-tance than the characters in it: in *Claire,* the principal character is at once a girl and a stream. Even the love affairs in each play are dominated by the natural setting, which gives them depth, specifi-city, and continuity.

The tone of Char's poetic theater and the feeling behind it are very close to those of J.M. Synge, whom he greatly admires. Com-pare, for instance, Synge's idea of a "serious" poetic drama — serious taken in the French sense, as he explains in his preface to *The Tinker's Wedding:*[2] "The drama is made serious ... by the degree in which it gives the nourishment, not very easy to define, on which our imaginations live." And, in his preface to the *Playboy of the Western World:*[3] "... in countries where the imagination of the people, and the language they use, is rich and living, it is possible for a writer to be rich and copious in his words, and at the same time to give the reality, which is the root of all poetry, in a compre-hensive and natural form." Against the "pallid and joyless" speech of some realist writers, Synge demands exactly the qualities we might find in Char's theater, based on the deep humor and natural poetry of the Provençal countryside: "On the stage one must have reality and one must have joy . . . the rich joy found only in what is superb and wild in reality. In a good play every speech should be as fully flavoured as a nut or apple, and such speeches cannot be written by anyone who works among people who have shut their lips on poetry." Synge's diatribe against dried-up "intellectualism" which has turned its back on popular concerns and lyricism is forceful in much the same way as Char's attack on those who choose a "ville sans plis" ("town without pleats"), for writers cannot accept identification with "places where the spring-time of the local life has been forgotten, and the harvest is a memory only, and the straw has been turned into bricks."[4]

A. Le Soleil des eaux (The Sun of Waters) (1946)

Char's first and best-known play is presented as a "spectacle for a fisherman's canvas." Its forty-two scenes in rapid succession build toward a political climax which is also a psychological one, for two moral concerns are intimately connected here, and Char's description might apply to both: "a poem, a drama, a plea, a lament." This passionate and tragic history of a river's pollution and its devastating effect on the fishermen living from it carries a general warning far beyond any ecological one, however serious, about the spoiling of pure things, about the necessity of retaining good and of refusing evil under whatever guise.

The poet's love of the Vaucluse is tacit here, but none the less evident. One of the epigraphs for the play comes from Petrarch, with whom the Fontaine de Vaucluse is linked, by fact and with affection: "In this refuge, there is no insolent citizen to challenge us, no flailing tongue to lacerate us. Neither disagreements, nor clamor, neither trial, nor din of war: neither avarice nor ambition nor envy are known there. . . . Everything speaks of joy, simplicity, freedom; it is a moderate state between poverty and riches. . . . In Vaucluse, the air is healthy, the winds temperate, the springs clear, the river full of fish" (TC, 79). The irony of the last statement in the light of the play's events is bitter: the action takes place in 1904, when the trout in the Sorgue began to die from the wastes poured into the river by a factory, where the director's sole concern is with efficiency. With minor changes, it could just as well be about any other of the possible menaces to an environment rich in poetry, some of which are specifically discussed in other chapters here, such as the atomic installations on the Mont Ventoux — on the heights of Albion — and so on. This particular pollution is drastic precisely because the fishermen of Saint-Laurent, granted their control over the river Sorgue by the popes of Avignon in the Middle Ages, had an abundance of fish to live on, with little else. The play, unliterary in style by intention, is partly a play of class against class, of factory owner against worker; it ends with an explosion set by the fishermen, but whose triumph is balanced by the death of one of their number.

The images are deliberately simple and appropriate to the nature of the play: in the introduction, trout are contrasted with eel in such a way that the former elicit our sympathy directly. The conviction of the entire work, originally performed for the radio, is such that, in an appendix ("The Why of *Le Soleil des eaux*"), a monologue of the only fisherman who was living at the time of writing, has a surprising actual strength. "You have to live with the fish," says Marius Dimier. And the play is written about just that as well, about the closeness of the human and animal worlds. Char explains there that he is calling on the resources of his fellow man, which the latter must not be shamed into leaving unused. His epoch is on trial, and he exemplifies evil and the opposition to it by means of these modest beings, close to the earth and to the water: "The face of daily bread, its direct need, gave to these men certain traits which were, I believe, human" (TC, 222). The play could have carried as an epigraph Char's own poem "La Truite,"[5] or, alternatively, any of the many passages on daily bread found elsewhere in his work, and invoked here also. As a simple representation of work in one common task, the making of bread reappears frequently, for its monetary worth is imperceptible, while its human value is irreplaceable.[6] In that, it resembles the fishermen.

The introduction stresses the unimportance of literature as weighed against ordinary language, and the importance, on the contrary, of emblems and images. The land of the poem is as fertile or as poor as its signs and its moral substance:

Here nothing should appear but certain indices of literature. The tongue of laziness and action, the language of daily bread is spoken, a language with no value.

Circumscribed, the eternal evil and the eternal good struggle there in the minimal figures of the trout and the eel. Fishermen bear their colors.

That the poem requires for its survival rich land and fallow earth is not ignored by anyone to whom certain exigencies matter. Still another armful of live wood, the last, and this mysterious common sense, fertile in drama, will disappear in smoke....

It is this significant and lost adventure that *The Sun of Waters* proposes to tell. (TC, 83)

The local color of the play is vivid, and at times the respect for local custom leads to certain awkwardnesses, as Char points out, commenting on the names of these fishermen. For example, many of the Saint-Laurent fishermen have Abondance[7] as a last name, so there are nicknames such as "grass snake" or "my nails" to differentiate them: the former, because of the nervous and supple character of the man, the second because of the knots on his neck.

The story, like the names, is veridical, and the tradition, long. A king of the river was always elected, to rule over disputes, a custom to which one of Char's poems in *La Nuit talismanique* refers: "Rex Fluminis Sorgiae." This natural and elected royalty makes, for those aware of the history, an ironic contrast with the artificial power of the factory director, as the common decency of the fisherman contrasts with his cruelty and insensitivity; the hard lines of the factory itself stand in sharp opposition to the fishermen's boats moving slowly up and down the river. These contrasts lie at the heart of the play, making up its canvas, which is also the net or *toile* of the fishermen, in which the play can be said to be caught. Other contrasts abound: the old armorer in conversation with the young hero, whose goodness in turn stands over against the slimy and eel-like character of the traitor; the young heroine in contrast to the older widow, and the great physical bulk of Louis Uni — called Apollon or Apollo for his remarkable physique — contrasted with the daintiness of his wife. Similarly, on the natural side, there are the contrasts of the trout against the eels, the rocks and river; and most important of all, the play of the one against the many. As in the frequent references to "certain beings" or "some chosen individuals" in Char's poems, one heroic individual may represent the many, whose strength is finally elicited by his own: "The dignity of one man alone isn't noticed. The dignity of a thousand men has a look of battle about it" (TC, 198). When the collective decision is taken to dynamite the factory, a fisherman is killed in the ensuing fight: "How can you know who will be killed in the hunting? How can you look ahead?" asks the armorer. The answer, by the heroine, is composed of another question: "Why look ahead?" Again we are reminded of the statement in *Aromates chasseurs:* "The interrogative answer is the answer of being." (AC, 18). The action remains open, as the deepest problem of the play is no nearer to a solution.

Attached to the play is an appendix of documents, bearing an epigraph from Ovid: "My book, you will go forth in that island, and you will go in that island without me" (TC, 211). Char speaks here of his reason for writing the play: he was asked to create a piece for a few men who read aloud to each other in the evening, in the region between the Sorgue and the Rhône rivers. The play, theatrical without appearing so, is supposed to be life multiplied two or three times, he says, but no more. It is, then, a starting point for the imagination rather than a literary resolution.

Poetry has its origin, he continues, in the dialogues of those beings who live close to the sketches of creation, not just close to its masterpieces. Their modesty protects them: "the almost constant menace of annihilation weighing on them is their surest safeguard. The apprenticeship of the poet in such company is a privileged apprenticeship." Even if the fishermen die out, the poet who has known them carries on, from his former lesson learned among them, something of their spirit. The regret not only of a bygone time but of a whole way of being is most eloquently stated by the fisherman already quoted, Marius Dimier: he laments not just the chlorine of the factories as it destroys but the casting lines which do not require the sensitivity of individual poles and lines, and the outsiders now permitted to join the fishing societies without having been steeped in the lore and the subtleties of the river. "You have to live with the fish. To tell you about the fishermen is to tell you about those who have now disappeared. I was the last. I no longer fish. . . . They have chased us from our river. . . . I don't go to my fishing hut any longer. I do an idiot's job just to eat. I am unhappy: I don't live with the fish any more" (TC, 218). And here it should be said, lest this seem only a lament of the past for the past, that in actuality another new factory has now been built, near the poet's town: its products have the same effect as those described in the play. It is, often, as if nothing were ever to be changed.

It may not be too farfetched to see here, in the uncomplicated transparency of this play, as simple as the sun on the waters, the same character as that shown in the speech of those beings who so fascinate Char, Les Transparents, those wandering poets who had no home but nature, who lived by acting and recounting tales, in the early days of the century. They were unique to the Vaucluse, and it is in their honor that the first texts of *Les Matinaux* were composed. One of them, Hubert le Transparent, gives the second epigraph to this play: "I am living. I love life. When I'm dead, Death will love me." The Transparents wrote for two people, as one of them said: "for myself and for nature." Their spirit is imperishable. We might think here of Char's statement about those beings of transparency, the recent people of morning: "The Matinals would exist even if the evening and the morning no longer existed" ("Faire du chemin avec...," 1976). An equal stylistic simplicity is visible in the two later plays, where nature takes a quieter role, but a no less essential one: first, a play concerning a mountain, and then one concerning a river. In each the humans and their destiny come under the sway of natural forces, to which they are bound by an almost mystical bond, inexplicable yet strongly sensed.

B. Sur les hauteurs (On the Heights) (1947)

Of the three plays, this one seems the lightest, by the intention of the poet. Char subtitles it "A passing inscription" and explains that it is made of twigs and thread, moss and dust, like a "nest suspended in the summer. Nothing else" (TC, 9). In its twelve scenes, a nocturnal setting predominates, so that nothing is clearly seen: even the climactic moment is glimpsed through a window, as if it might be a dream. The castle of Aulan in the Drôme is plunged into an initial darkness, its own and that of the neighboring mountain, and the play will end at night also. Two boys, watching the castle and a couple at a lighted window, speak of their desire for it to be night always, and a particular nocturnal intensity is felt here: it is clear that the darkness is as symbolic as it is actual, that it serves legend, myth, and the marvelous in this play situated not just on the heights of a mountain (specifically called Mont Ventoux, in an addition to the proofs) but on some highest point of fantasy.

A seventeen year old ventures into the deserted castle and finds a girl dressed as she might have been long ago, called simply The Unknown One, a spirit from the castle's past. Their love is threatened not only by an actual impossibility but by a verbal inscription, a message carved on the chimney. The message serves as the psychological center of the play: "If you are, oh my Beloved, on the heights,/Give me wings to reach you." The girl warns, in response to the inscription, that the mountain will not permit their happiness: "Woe to those in love, if they have a height above their love." (Char's poem "Sur les hauteurs" is a briefer example of his own — and, by a sure contagion, his reader's — involvement with height.)[8] Only children under a charm should be allowed to see them, says the boy; at that moment one of the children watching them is summoned home. The couple steps to the lighted window, toward the tragedy the play has been building up to predictably. An old man, who chases rabbits, thinking them the fairies who took away his parents long ago, opens fire on the window, and the girl falls, forever. "I loved Aulan," sobs the little boy. As the waters of the Sorgue in *Le Soleil des eaux* represent more than a river polluted, so the daughter of the legend in the castle of Aulan represents more than a single loss: the boy's lament reaches to every hope and every legend destroyed by reality.

These mountainous heights are very different from those in *L'Abominable des neiges*: far more real and still more threatening to human love. The myth of Venus come to earth, with all the equipment of science fiction, is on another level from this legend attached to an old castle, and it engages us less.

C. Claire (1948)

Throughout this strictly organized play in ten tableaux, the presence of Claire — a girl but also a stream — is felt. The epigraph is a fisherman's song:

> I was in love with a river and could not make her love me.
> For whom are you saving yourself, lovely one?
> Follow me and you'll find out.
>
> (TC, 39)

This figure of Claire comes partly from Artine,[9] who was dream and also transparency, who was "fraîche" in the double sense intended here also — cool, fresh, and young, a river and also a fire — and partly through numerous other figures and guises at other moments. Water stands out always by its generosity, its offering, and its suffering, by its clarity as by its *depth:* see the poems "La Sorgue," "Les Premiers instants," "Yvonne," and the title poem of *Le Nu perdu,* beginning: "They shall bear branches ... who raise from the well...," " as well as the tragic brevity of "Tracé sur le gouffre," and also the figures of Mary Magdalene and of the Buveuse, and the statue of Eve at Autun. All these figures and texts finally participate in the act of poetry as it is seen at last, with an unparticularized "other hand" holding the candle and bringing the inspiration of night. The nocturnal river of *La Nuit talismanique* flows by as if it would redeem the formerly sterile, like the flow liberated by love in *Le Visage nuptial,* the amorous gesture conquering the desert sand. This constant renewal of poetry is given figure and visibility in a feminine inspiration, again taken in both senses: as spirit and as source. The traits change slightly according to the guises, as in the tableaux of *Claire,* but the essential attributes of water remain. (As we have pointed out, this entire discussion could have been situated in the preceding chapter, dealing with the element of water.)

In a commentary on *Claire,* reprinted in *Recherche de la base et du sommet,* Char speaks of inspiration, of clarity, and of a stream: "...the stream I recount is made up of many Claires. They love, dream, wait, suffer, question, hope, work. They are lovely or pale, often both, attached to the fate of each; avid for life" (TC, 37). In the entire play, only Claire is named, the other characters serving only as a backdrop for her action. In the opening scene, a mushroom picker climbs the rocks near the spring into which he plunges his arms and then falls motionless. Already the scene is disquieting: is the fall an accident or provoked by his pride in climbing? or a revenge wreaked by the landscape on the despoiler of nature? When Claire, in a girl's voice, declares her origin and her ubiquitous being, the latter seems the most probable of the solutions: she was born of the violent love of clouds and glaciers, it is said. She is everywhere and transparent: seeing her life will help us discover our own, as "L'Homme à la peau de miroir" was to reflect our own inner personage in his surface, or again, as Artine the river was said to be our transparent guide to the country of our own fate. There is a basic complicity between the stream and ourselves: "Through my eyes, you will reconsider some moments you participate in hastily, or against whose meaning you rebelled. In reliving them, you may feel that anguish or that happiness which are only bearable in dreams" (TC, 43).

Claire is transparency itself, and youthfulness, like Artine. Hence her name, indicating freshness as well as luminosity and an untroubled nature. And yet she is born again in every moment and in all conditions, of which the play will show us a sampling, incomprehensible without this prologue: "I have just been born. Claire is my name.... Why is it impossible to embrace this instant always? Scarcely do I have the time to experience my youth, to show you yours, than we fly together toward tortures, but also toward the great prologues full of hope" (TC, 44). In the ensuing tableaux — disconnected except by her presence, in order for her importance to be made clear — various girls carry in their bearing or their attitude the marks of a stream. First, the wife of the wounded mushroom picker, confides that one never marries the person one loves: we hear her name only at the conclusion of the scene and then the river sound rushes by, a sound recurring at the end of the majority of scenes. Next Claire is seen as the servant in a bourgeois family, then bringing water to a table of peasants in whose family she seems to belong, then throwing herself into a river over an unhappy love affair.

The scenes continue thus, and finally a child will be fathered by a glacier and a great river: here the birth of Claire is predicted, an event we recognize from the prologue, where a child will be born of a glacier and a cloud: "What name shall we give it?/A name not somber? That name must exist!" A fine rain announces the coming birth, and the poet writes of sharing and of happiness, and of a source. Here the element of water once more predominates, as it does in the long course of Char's work, now visible, now not. Finally, an old man, described by his son as generous, as perpetual (here we think of the distinction Char draws between the eternal and the perpetual, giving his preference to the latter, as he would to a perpetual source), turns to the stream and asks it, as his daughter, to help him: we assume this to be the glacier's request to the clear-flowing water, and we feel the request is granted. The limpid water and the river with silt are said to merge in marriage, forever. The river speaks in a man's voice, responding now to the voice of the girl or the stream which opened the play: "Claire, let me guide you now. Mingle your body with mine.... You are no longer isolated in the folds of the earth and I am no longer alone before time, before the night" (TC, 76). The union of the male and female elements ends the play thus, in stability and in motion, after Claire's various transpositions like so many phases of a cycle.

Not only is the ambivalence of this greater than that of any other of Char's spectacles, but the figure described by *Claire* — a figure at once geometrical, psychological, moral, and theatrical — is as subtle as it is omnipresent. Themes from the other spectacles merge here and from other of Char's works, sometimes in prefiguration and sometimes in echo. We have seen in *La Conjuration* the image of the swift falling to his doom from the slightest wound in his heart, and we have also seen it in *Sur les hauteurs,* a poem of the same name. From *Le Soleil des eaux,* the river Sorgue is present again throughout the meditations of *La Nuit talismanique;* these examples could be multiplied, since many of Char's texts refer to themselves as well as to the things beyond. Yet *Claire* seems to be situated at the center of a major line in Char's poetic work: "Will you find someone today to talk to, by whose side you can be refreshed? . . . Against today's hostility we play the card of *Claire.* And if we lose, we shall play the card of *Claire* again. Our trump cards are perpetual, like the storm and the kiss, the fountains and the wounds washed there" (TC, 38).

III   *The Clear Season*

And so it is appropriate that the images of the other plays should appear here also, sometimes foreshadowing and sometimes in retrospect. Claire, the name and the play as well, have the limpidity, and the ambivalence of the snow in *L'Abominable des neiges,* this clarity and this transparency complementary to its cold opacity: nor is her glacial origin unrelated to the snow. The mirror of the hero in *La Conjuration* is included here, in Claire's mirroring of her audience, in her discovering of our character as we discovers hers. Her brilliance is in the gully sparkling after the rain in the poem "Traverse," the shaft of sunlight protecting the young man in *L'Homme qui marchait dans un rayon de soleil,* and her liquid transparency and optimism shine already in *Le Soleil des eaux.* She combines fire and water, sun and freshness. The river and the rain running through *La Conjuration* and initially eulogized there at the opening and the close, the river Sorgue in *Le Soleil des eaux,* the rain of *L'Homme qui marchait:* these watery images, like their snowy counterpart, proliferate in the spectacles, seen under the trees of this seasonal theater, lasting the six years from 1946 to 1952, but seen again and reflected upon.

In the dry land of the Vaucluse, sunlight is everywhere available and water has a special value attached to it. The "bare land" at the summits of its mountains — "sur les hauteurs" — is redeemed by the liquid images, or by the miraculous snow, as its transposition. *Claire* is, even before her union with the masculine principle of the river, made for "great prologues full of hope." Her flow represents an elusive moment, bright with optimism, but also with the essential youth of poetry and spectacle, whose outer realization in the various moments of these plays conforms to an inner reality, as Claire's various guises mirror our own. The cyclical working out of births and sources, the convergence of stream and river and sea, the profile of the mountain heights and of village squares, the shifting of night to day to twilight, from past to present: the tapestry of all these spectacles is variegated but not densely textured. In it all, the relation of human life to natural surroundings is closely felt, effectively illuminating that relationship in Char's poems, where it is often more elliptical than here. The fabric woven or the canvas painted, that is, the *toile* of *Le Soleil des eaux,* serves as the background for other spectacles, and the threads go to make up other texts also, whether of an exterior or an interior architecture, whether of a mental theater or a real one — under the trees, for a summer season, and for later seasons still to come.

CHAPTER 6

Conclusion

CHAR'S importance for contemporary poetry cannot be too strongly stated. The intensity of his writing, the essential gravity of his tone, the extent of his moral concern demand a more arduous attention than that we bring to most other poets: to Saint-John Perse, for example, or Apollinaire. Char's exigencies toward the reader are in fact close to those of Mallarmé. The same is true of the almost insuperable difficulty of translation which confronts us in the case of Char: nowhere else is the "indomitable genius of the French language" felt in quite the same way.[1] This is not a cause for despair but rather a reason for further efforts. If this book ends on a note of optimism, the reason is similar — the presence of a great poet, no matter how discouraging to those who would prefer to analyze always with some certainty of satisfactory comprehension — calls for reflection on the joys of multiplicity and of mystery. Precisely because all cannot be stated once and for all, "The best work is the one which keeps its secret the longest."[2] One would not choose, then, to explain the secret of Char's poetry, even if one could, but only to point out its nature, and, insofar as possible, a few possible ways of contemplating its profundity.

Char's Vaucluse continues the tradition of Petrarch and yet extends, as we have said elsewhere,[3] not only into the world far beyond, but also and especially into the interior setting which we can share with him. The geography, specific and local, is finally transmuted into a more invisible sense of place. Openness becomes identical with enclosure: Char's room — glimpsed in *La Nuit talismanique,* with its lighted candle, his book and writing instruments, the mystery of the surroundings as if another creation were contained in this one — is familiar to us from Mallarmé's *Igitur.* But in this room and beyond it are other presences and innumerable other passages. . . .

Reading Char's poetry, we never cease to be aware of the importance of the multiple, as each interpretation calls for another, as the poems have a changing resonance, collective and singular. The

154

reader's perspective shifts, as the poet relocates the lines in succeeding poems, the poems in succeeding volumes, and the volumes in succeeding collections; so the poet changes for us, and our involvement is correspondingly modified, if never lessened. And the texts teach us a lesson for the setting, which also is seen in different lightings and from different approaches.

Each place opens onto another: as if beyond the "Mirage des aiguilles," there were to be another kind of mirage, and as if, higher still than the lost city of Aerea, there were to be another lost city. I have spoken here of text and morality, of geography and architecture, of elements and of spectacle, and attempted, for each of these, to show an exterior aspect and an interior one, the latter not always explicitly stated, yet underlying the discussion and underlining parts of it. For the essential strength of this poetry does not lie only where it might seem to at first, but also elsewhere, at another depth entirely. The definition of that other level may change and indeed will change according to various readings it summons. The reading offered here is meant, in part, as a starting point for an interior journey, even as it seems to take the form of a conclusion.

Notes and References

Preface

1. Translated and edited by Mary Ann Caws and Jonathan Griffin; when the same text is used, the translations in the present volume conform to those in the Princeton edition. JG refers to Griffin's translations.

Chapter One

1. NT — *La Nuit talismanique.*
2. SP — *Sur la poésie.*
3. LM — *Les Matinaux.* Annotation in Doucet library.
4. A — *Arsenal.*
5. In the Fonds René Char-Yvonne Zervos of the Bibliothèque littéraire Jacques Doucet. MM — *Le Marteau sans maître.*
6. RBS — *Recherche de la base et du sommet.*
7. As Hölderlin puts it, the gods choose to hurl their lightning toward the being they privilege. See the later discussions on Hölderlin and the gods' election of the poet, in chapter 2 and *passim.* The information on Hölderlin comes principally from *Friedrich Hölderlin, Poems and Fragments* (Ann Arbor: University of Michigan Press, 1967), ed. and tr. Michael Hamburger.
8. Michel Carrouges, *André Breton et les données fondamentales du surréalisme* (Paris: Gallimard, 1950).
9. Cahiers de l'Herne, no. René Char, 1971. For instance, among the most valuable and touching comments are those by William Carlos Williams, who also contributes a poem.
10. Jean Starobinski, "René Char et la définition du poème," Courrier du Centre International d'Etudes poétiques, 66, Maison Internationale de la poésie, Brussels. Reprinted as the preface to *Ritorno sopramonte,* Vittorio Sereni's translations of Char's poems under the title *Retour amont* (Lo Specchio: Mondadori, 1973).
11. AC — *Aromates chasseurs.* (Not yet translated.)
12. In *The Presence of René Char* we discussed at some length the transposition of Char's "Parole en archipel" ("word as archipelago") to its reverse image in the nighttime sky.
13. FM — *Fureur et mystère.* Originally the title of this volume, perhaps Char's best-known work, was to be translated as *Rage and Mystery,*

but it was decided, by the poet, that *fureur* has more properly the sense of fury or of furor.

14. Translated as *Leaves of Hypnos* by Jackson Matthews in *Hypnos Waking* (New York: Random House, 1956).

15. André Breton, *Les Pas perdus* (Paris: Gallimard, 1924), pp. 7–8.

16. Pierre de Missac, "Situation de l'aphorisme," *Critique,* no. 323 (April, 1974).

17. NP — *Le Nu perdu.*

Chapter Two

1. See the "Note to Francis Curel" in Chapter One.

2. For example, see the large volume of original works by his friends the artists and the accompanying texts: *Le Monde de l'Art n'est pas le monde du pardon* (Paris: Maeght, 1975). Preface by Jacques Dupin.

3. Tristan Tzara, "Note sur la poésie," in *Sept manifestes Dada, suivis de lampisteries* (Paris: Pauvert, 1963).

4. Paul Valéry, *Oeuvres,* vol. I, Pléiade edition (Paris: Gallimard, 1957), p. 862.

5. Ibid.

6. E. H. Gombrich, "The Subject of Poussin's Orion," in *Symbolic Images: Studies in the Art of the Renaissance* (New York: Phaidon, 1972), in particular, pp. 121–22. See also Claude Simon, *Orion aveuglé* (Geneva: Skira, 1970).

7. See Sereni, (Chapter One, note 10). All the notes in this book are invaluable.

8. Thomas Hines, "L'Ouvrage de tous les temps, admiré: *Lettera amorosa*/René Char and Georges Braque," *Bulletin du Bibliophile,* no. 1, 1973.

9. *Se rencontrer paysage avec Joseph Sima,* exhibition Château de Ratilly, June 23 to September 16, 1973.

10. Mallarmé's *Igitur,* referred to above in the same connection, is an excellent example of the shadowy play of ambiguity. The comparison with the table and its open book, the candle about to be snuffed out, and the atmosphere of midnight is worth considering. "C'est le rêve pur d'un Minuit, en soi disparu, et dont la Clarté reconnue, qui seule demeure au sein de son accomplissement plongé dans l'ombre, résume sa stérilité sur la pâleur d'un livre ouvert que présente la table..." (Pléiade edition, p. 435). In Char and in Mallarmé, the figures of the unicorn and the ancient gods, and in both breath and life play against the dark, as speech against silence and chance against necessity: "Il ferme le livre — souffle la bougie — de son souffle qui contenait le hasard..." (Ibid., p. 442).

11. Sereni, p. 217: "Le Tricheur à l'as de carreau," "Rixe de

musiciens," "La Diseuse de bonne aventure," "Le Vielleur," are the four works of Georges de La Tour to which Char refers here. "For the oppositions and on the cohabitation of a 'diurnal' painter and a 'nocturnal' one (two times, two manners and thus two languages) the scheme of distinctions essential in the art of Georges de La Tour...," Sereni refers us to the catalog of the La Tour exhibition in the Orangerie (May 10 - September 25, 1972).

12. This statement is a response to and consolation for any translator or critic about to lose one of the meanings of a poem: Char uses it in just that way.

13. See "Evadé d'archipel" in *Aromates chasseurs,* in which Orion represents the figure of the poet, who escapes eventually both from his constellation and from our earth; he is essential, and not to be pinned down to one locality.

14. See note eight above.

15. Valéry, p. 562.

Chapter Three

1. The relationship between the two poets was a close one: it was by Eluard that the younger poet, whose *Arsenal* Eluard had read, was introduced to the Surrealists. A poetic portrait of Eluard is to be found in "Convergence des multiples."

2. We think also of the lamp and the table in Baudelaire's "Le Voyage," in Rimbaud's "Enfance," and in Mallarmé's "Brise Marine," and, as we comment, in many of Reverdy's poems.

3. Organized by Yvonne Zervos, Char's longtime friend, the friend of many artists and poets, whom she helped and encouraged.

4. Mary Ann Caws, *The Presence of René Char* (Princeton, N.J.: Princeton University Press, 1976). *Poems of René Char,* translated and annotated by Mary Ann Caws and Jonathan Griffin (Princeton, N.J.: Princeton University Press, 1976).

5. René Char, *Poètes d'aujourd'hui,* ed. Pierre Berger (Paris: Seghers, 1951).

Chapter Four

1. Gaston Bachelard, *La Psychanalyse du feu* (Paris: Gallimard, 1938); *L'Eau et les rêves* (Paris: Corti, 1942); *L'Air et les songes* (Paris: Corti, 1943); *La Terre et les rêveries de la volonté* (Paris: Corti, 1948); and *La Terre et les rêveries du repos* (Paris: Corti, 1948); *La Flamme d'une chandelle* (Paris: P.U.F., 1961).

2. Here we are thinking of such works as Maryvonne Meuraud's

study, *L'Image végétale dans la poésie d'Eluard* (Paris: Lettres Modernes, 1966).

3. As he declares in an interview with Christofides, quoted in Caws, *Surrealism and the Literary Imagination* (The Hague: Mouton, 1966).

4. Fonds René Char — Yvonne Zervos, no. 684, AE–IV–4.

5. Later to become the poem "Jouvence," in *Premières alluvions,* found in *Art bref, suivi de Premières alluvions* (*Brief Art, followed by First Alluvia*), G.L.M., 1950.

Jouvence

Ceux qui partent pour les* nuages
Se séparent de leur raison
La mer ouverte à l'oeil unique
Est leur taciturne horizon.

Youthfulness

Those who depart for the clouds
Leave their reason behind
The sea open to the lone eye
Is their taciturn horizon.

*The poet has corrected the printing error of the first line: "aux nuages" to read "pour les nuages."

6. Mircea Eliade, *Forgerons et alchimistes* (Paris: Flammarion, 1956).

7. Yvonne Zervos: see above, chapter 3, note three.

8. See our discussion of "Fastes" in *The Presence of René Char.*

9. André Spire, *Vers les routes absurdes* (Paris: Mercure de France, 1911), passim, or see Stanley Burnshaw, *André Spire and his Poetry* (Philadelphia: Centaur, 1933).

10. Char made the changes in the first edition of *Les Matinaux* himself, in the copy held by the Bibliothèque littéraire Jacques Doucet, 722.18.

11. Correspondence with Jonathan Griffin.

12. Correspondence with the author.

13. James Lawler, "Le Taureau" et "La Truite," *Le Siècle éclaté: dada, surréalisme et avant-gardes,* no. 1, Lettres Modernes, Minard, pp. 193–99. English version in *About French Poetry from Dada to "Tel Quel": Text and Theory,* ed. Caws (Detroit: Wayne State, 1975). See also the article of Jean Starobinski in *Liberté,* Hommage à René Char, vol. 1, no. 4 (July–August, 1968).

14. Photographs of all three manuscripts in *The Presence of René Char.*

15. In manuscript, no. 759, AE–IV–22.

16. The sirocco left by the former gods has now become only a "fresh breath."

17. "Mémorial" óf Pascal, *Oeuvres*, ed. Brunschwicg (Paris: Hachette, 1930), p. 142.

18. For Poussin's canvas and Gombrich's comment, see above, chapter 2, note 6.

19. Compare the brutality of the following line from "Aux Portes d'Aerea": "Visé par l'abeille de fer, la rose en larmes s'est ouverte" (NP, 19). So civilization destroys nature.

20. Fonds René Char — Yvonne Zervos, no. 830, AE–IV–7 bis.

21. (New York: Atheneum, 1972).

22. E. Tesauro, *Il Cannochiale Aristotelico* (Venice, 1655), quoted in *The Flaming Heart* by Mario Praz (New York: Doubleday, 1958), p. 224.

Chapter Five

1. TC — *Trois Coups sous les arbres.*

2. J.M. Synge, *Four Plays and the Aran Islands* (London: Oxford University Press, 1962), p. 41.

3. Ibid., pp. 75-6.

4. Ibid., p. 76.

5. "La Truite" (LM, 107).

6. See the Cycle of Bread, in Caws, *The Presence of René Char.*

7. Thus, *Abondance viendra* in *Le Marteau sans maître* has the name of one of that family, who worked for Char's grandmother, and had no richness besides his name and his many children.

8. "Sur les hauteurs" (LM, 45).

9. A figure studied at length in *The Presence of René Char;* see the chapter on *Artine* and *La Nuit talismanique.*

Chapter Six

1. As Helen Vendler points out: for her help in the translation of a few difficult passages, I am enormously grateful.

2. Valéry, I, 562.

3. See the preface to *Poems of René Char.*

Selected Bibliography

PRIMARY SOURCES

Unless otherwise stated, place of publication is Paris. An asterisk indicates works included in one of the popular current editions.

Les Cloches sur le coeur. Editions Le Rouge et Le Noir, 1928.
Arsenal. Privately printed, 1929.
Artine. Editions surréalistes, 1930.
Ralentir travaux (in collaboration with Breton and Eluard). Editions surréalistes, 1930.
Le Tombeau des Secrets. Nîmes, 1930.
L'Action de la justice est éteinte. Editions surréalistes, 1931.
Le Marteau sans maître. Corti, 1934.
Placard pour un chemin des écoliers. G.L.M., 1937.
Dehors la nuit est gouvernée. G.L.M., 1938.
Seuls demeurent. Gallimard, 1945.
Feuillets d'Hypnos. Gallimard, 1946.
Le Poème pulvérisé. Editions Fontaine, 1946.
*Fureur et mystère** (collected edition). Gallimard, 1948.
Le Soleil des eaux. Librairie Matarasso, 1949.
Art bref, suivi de Premières alluvions. G.L.M., 1950.
Les Matinaux. Gallimard, 1950.
A une sérénité crispée. Gallimard, 1951.
La Paroi et la prairie. G.L.M., 1952.
Le Rempart de brindilles. Louis Broder, 1952.
A la santé du serpent. G.L.M., 1954.
*Recherche de la base et du sommet.** Gallimard, 1955, followed by *Pauvreté et privilège** (collected edition [prose texts]). Gallimard, 1955.
Les Compagnons dans le jardin. Louis Broder, 1956.
Poèmes et proses choisis. Gallimard, 1957.
L'Inclémence lointaine. Pierre Berès, 1961.
*La Parole en archipel,** (with *Les Matinaux*). Gallimard, 1962.
Lettera amorosa. Gallimard, 1963.
Commune présence. Gallimard, 1964.
Retour amont. G.L.M., 1965
Trois Coups sous les arbres, Théâtre saisonnier (collected edition of theater). Gallimard, 1967.

163

Les Transparents. Alès: P.A.B., 1967.
Dans la pluie giboyeuse. Gallimard, 1968.
L'Effroi la joie. Jean Hugues, 1971.
Le Nu perdu. Gallimard, 1972.
La Nuit talismanique. Skira, 1972.
Le Monde de l'art n'est pas le monde du pardon. Maeght, 1975.
Aromates chasseurs. Gallimard, 1975.

Principal Translations

in English:

Hypnos Waking. Translated by Jackson Matthews, with William Carlos
    Williams, Richard Wilbur, William Jay Smith, Barbara Howes, W.S.
    Merwin, and James Wright. Collection of major poems. New York:
    Random House, 1956.
Leaves of Hypnos (translation of *Feuillets d'Hypnos*). Translated by Cid
    Corman. New York: Grossman, 1975.
Poems of René Char. Translated and annotated by Mary Ann Caws and
    Jonathan Griffin. Contains a large variety of poems, selected in
    collaboration with   René Char. Princeton: Princeton University
    Press, 1976.

in German:

Dichtungen. Translated by Paul Celan, Johannes Hübner, Lothar
    Klünner, and Jean-Pierre Wilhelm. Preface by Albert Camus. Frank-
    furt am Main: S. Fischer Verlag, 1959.
Hypnos und Andere Dichtungen. Translated by Paul Celan, Johannes
    Hübner, Lothar Klünner, Jean-Pierre Wilhelm, and Franz Wurm.
    Frankfurt am Main: S. Fischer Verlag, 1963.
Dichtungen II. Translated by Gerd Henninger, Johannes Hübner, and
    Lothar Klünner. Frankfurt am Main: S. Fischer Verlag, 1968.

in Italian:

Poesia e Prosa. Translated by Giorgio Caproni and Vittorio Sereni. Milan:
    Feltrinelli, 1962.
Ritorno Sopramonte (translation of *Retour amont*). Translated and anno-
    tated by Vittorio Sereni. Preface by Jean Starobinski (translation of
    "René Char et la définition du poème," Courrier du Centre Interna-
    tional d'Études Poétiques, 66, Maison Internationale de la poésie,
    Brussels, 1968). Lo Specchio: Mondadori, 1973.

in Spanish:

Antologia. Translated by Raül Gustavo Aguirre. Buenos Aires: Ediciones
    del Mediodia, 1968.

Hojas de Hipnos (1943–1944) (translation of *Feuillets d'Hypnos*). Translated by Edison Simons. Madrid: Visor, 1973.

in Roumanian:
Poeme Alese. Translated by Gellu Naum. Editura Tineretului, 1968.

in Polish:
Wspólna obecność (Selected Poems). Translated by Artur Miedzyrzecki. Warsaw: Panstworvy Instytut Wydawniczy, 1971.

in Dutch:
Samen aanwezig: Gedichten 1930–1972. Translated by C.P. Heering-Moorman. Amsterdam: Meulenhoff.

in Serbo-Croat:
Poezija. Translated by Petar Šegedin, Oto Šolc, Grigor Vitez. Zagreb: Mladost, 1963.

in Russian:
A choice of poems, translated by Vadim Kozovoí. Moscow, 1973.

SECONDARY SOURCES

1. Books and prefaces

René Char's Poetry. Studies by Maurice Blanchot, Gabriel Bounoure, Albert Camus, Georges Mounin, Gaëtan Picon, René Ménard, James Wright. Editions de Luca, Italy, 1956. In English.

BARELLI, JACQUES. *L'Écriture de René Char.* La Pensée universelle, 1973.

BERGER, PIERRE. Preface to *René Char.* Seghers, Coll. Poètes d'aujourd'hui, 1951.

BLANCHOT, MAURICE. *La Bête de Lascaux.* G.L.M., 1958. Eloquent study of silence in a "work speaking to us from far off but with an intimate understanding which brings it near to us," of a "future word" available in the present, of a purity and a mystery which it is not the task of the critic to clarify.

BLIN, GEORGES. Preface to *Commune présence.* Gallimard, 1964. Lapidary expression as it is related to the poem in archipelago form; the separated Greek islands are seen as images of scintillation and syncopation against the background of an enduring grandeur.

CAWS, MARY ANN and GRIFFIN, JONATHAN. Prefaces to *Poems of René Char.* Princeton University Press, 1976. Relation to specific geography of Char's Vaucluse to the wider place of the poem; studies of certain problems in translating a poet "literally" and with his collaboration.

CAWS, MARY ANN. *The Presence of René Char.* Princeton University Press, 1976. Illustration of differing techniques in reading this poetry and in the shifting perspectives imposed by successive re-readings, in which the critic becomes the "mortal partner" and the "loyal adversary" of the poet.

DUPIN, JACQUES. Preface to *Le Monde de l'Art n'est pas le monde du pardon.* Maeght, 1975. Poetic eulogy of Char as seer.

FOURCADE, DOMINIQUE. Preface to *Cahier de l'Herne,* no. 1, René Char, 1971. Introduction to this poet "unequaled and alone among us."

GUERRE, PIERRE. Preface to *René Char.* Seghers, coll. Poètes d'aujourd'hui, 1961.

LA CHARITÉ, VIRGINIA. *The Poetry and Poetics of René Char.* University of North Carolina Studies in Romance Languages and Literatures, Chapel Hill, 1968.

MÉNARD, RENÉ. *Cinq essais pour interpréter René Char.* "La Condition poétique," NRF, coll. Espoir, 1959. On the "writing of a presence."

MOUNIN, GEORGES. *Avez-vous lu Char?,* 1947, with *La Communication poétique,* Gallimard, 1969. Char's "most tenacious search for the most absolute totality," the poem as the highest silence, as a motion toward absence, as "poetry in itself."

RAU, GRETA. *René Char ou la Poésie accrue.* Corti, 1957. On Char's "mental light," on time and simultaneity.

SERENI, VITTORIO. Introduction to *Ritorno, sopramonte,* Italian translation of *Retour amont* with notes. Lo Specchio, Mondadori, 1975.

STAROBINSKI, JEAN. Preface to above: Italian translation of "René Char et la définition du poème," also appearing in *Liberté,* Hommage à René Char, vol. 1, no. 4 (July–August, 1968) and in Courrier du Centre International d'Etudes Poétiques, no. 66. Brussels, 1968.

2. Special numbers of journals

L'Arc: René Char. (no. 22). Aix-en-Provence, 1963. Articles by Jean Beaufret, Maurice Blanchot, Georges Blin, Georges Poulet, Jacques Dupin, C.A. Hackett and others.

Cahiers de l'Herne: René Char. Studies and letters, poems by Saint-John Perse, William Carlos Williams, Martin Heidegger, Paul Eluard, Pierre Reverdy, Albert Camus, Octavio Paz, Dominique Fourcade, Georges Bataille, Yves Battistini, Maurice Blanchot, Gaëtan Picon and others. Paris, 1971.

Liberté: Hommage à René Char. Studies by Jean Starobinski, Yves Battistini, Dominique Fourcade, Pierre-André Benoit and others.

World Literature Today. Special number in honor of René Char. Studies by a wide range of critics in English.

3. Selected Studies and articles (including a few in French)

BATAILLE, GEORGES. "Lettre à René Char sur les incompatabilités de l'écrivain," in *Botteghe Oscure,* no. VI, Fall, 1950 (ed. Marguerite Gaetani). Answer to Char's questionnaire: "Y a-t-il des incompati-bilités?" in *Empédocle* (RBS, 36). Reprinted in *L'Herne.*

BATTISTINI, YVES. "Pour un climat autour de René Char et l'esquisse d'un portrait par-delà les temps," *L'Herne.* Supposing that we were to find fragments of Char's work like those from Heraclitus. . . .

BLANCHOT, MAURICE. "René Char et la pensée du neutre," *L'Arc.* The notion of the grammatically unspecified, leaving open the categories of subject and object to create another sort of relation, as in Hera-clitus and Heidegger.

BLIN, GEORGES. "L'Instant multiple dans la poésie de René Char," *L'Arc.* Relation to Greek thought, to sudden illuminations and constant intermittencies.

CAWS, MARY ANN. "The Poetics of a Surrealist Passage and Beyond," *Twentieth Century Literature,* Surrealism issue, vol. 21, Feb. 1975, no. 1. Passage by fire in Breton and Char.

CRANSTON, MECHTHILD. *Enfance, ô mon amour: Apollinaire, Saint-John Perse, et René Char,* Nouvelles Editions Debresse, 1970.

———. "René Char, 1923-1928: The Young Poet's Struggle for Com-munication," *PMLA,* vol. 87, no. 5, no. 72.

———. *"Arrière-Histoire du Poème pulvérisé:* René Char's *Winterreise,"* French Review, vol. XLVII (special issue, no. 5, Spring, 1973).

———. "Violence and Magic: Aspects of René Char's Surrealist Appren-ticeship," *Forum for Modern Language Studies,* vol. X, no. 1, Jan. 1974.

———. "L'Homme du matin et . . . .Celui des Ténèbres. Char, Rimbaud: Parallels and Contrasts," *Kentucky Romance Quarterly,* Fall, 1974.

FESTA MCCORMICK, DIANA. "A***," *French Review,* vol. XLVI (special issue, no. 5, Spring, 1973).

HINES, THOMAS. "'L'Ouvrage de tout temps admiré,' Georges Braque et René Char," *Bibliophile,* no. 1, 1973.

JACKSON, ELIZABETH R. *Worlds Apart: Structural Parallels in the Poetry of Paul Valéry, Saint-John Perse, Benjamin Péret, and René Char.* (The Hague: Mouton, 1976).

KERNO, JACQUES. "L'Oeuvre de René Char en 1966," *Commerce,* no. 17, Spring, 1967.

LA CHARITÉ, VIRGINIA. "The Role of Rimbaud in Char's Poetry," *PMLA,* Jan. 1974, no. 1.

———. "Surrealist Patterns in René Char's 'Eaux-Mères,' " *Dada/Surrealism,* no. 2, 1972.

———. "Beyond the Poem: René Char's *La Nuit talismanique,*" *Symposium,* Spring, 1976.

LA PORTE, ROGER. "Clarté de René Char," *Critique,* June, 1965. On suffering and art as "the duty of a prince."

LAUDE, JEAN. "Trois Figures pour René Char," *Liberté,* Hommage à René Char (July–August, 1968), vol. 10, no. 4. Confrontation and ascent; the leap as opposed to the path.

LAWLER, JAMES. "René Char's 'Quatre fascinants,'" in *About French Poetry from Dada to "Tel Quel": Text and Theory,* ed. Mary Ann Caws, Detroit, Wayne State, 1975. (French version in *Le Siècle éclaté,* [Minard] no. 1, 1974.

MAYER, FRANZ. "René Char et Hölderlin," *L'Herne.* The poetic function as conceived by the two poets.

DE MISSAC, PIERRE. "Situation de l'aphorisme," *Critique,* no. 323 (April, 1974). On aphoristic form as oracular and gnomic, befitting the seer.

ONIMUS, JEAN. "René Char," in *Expérience de la poésie.* Desclée De Brouwer, 1973. Main currents of Char's writing, morality, and poetics.

POULET, GEORGES. "René Char: De la constitution à la dissémination," *L'Arc.* On the convergence of wartime events and poetic choice: the understanding in the latter "precedes even the appearance of the circumstance and ... remains in the poem as in the poet's mind ... when other events have succeeded it."

RICHARD, JEAN-PIERRE. "René Char," in *Onze Études sur la poésie moderne.* Seuil, 1964. Thematic study of contrasts: of the images of morning with "negative existence," of the fluid or "antistatic" with the explosive, of the instantaneous with the enduring.

WISE, SUSAN. *La Notion de poésie chez André Breton et René Char.* Aix-en-Provence: Publication des Annales de la Faculté des Lettres, 1968.

Index